Elders in Rebellion

A GUIDE TO SENIOR ACTIVISM

Lou Cottin

ANCHOR PRESS/DOUBLEDAY
GARDEN CITY, NEW YORK
1979

The Anchor Press Edition is the first publication of *Elders in Rebellion*.
Anchor Press Edition: 1979

ISBN: 0-385-14486-5
Library of Congress Catalog Card Number: 14486-5
Copyright © 1979 by Louis M. Cottin
All Rights Reserved
Printed in the United States of America
First Edition

Library of Congress Cataloging in Publication Data

Cottin, Lou.
  Elders in rebellion.

  1. Aged—United States—Social conditions.
2. Age discrimination—United States. 3. Old
age assistance—United States. I. Title.
HQ1064.U5C622   301.43′5′0973

To Nikka Nagourney Cottin.
This book, which you have
titled so aptly, gives me
the opportunity to tell the
world publicly,

I Love You

Lou Cottin

Contents

Preface

By Congressman Claude Pepper,
Chairman of the Select Committee on Aging,
U. S. House of Representatives

I personally have read many of Lou Cottin's newspaper columns devoted to the elderly, their problems, and what is being done about them and what isn't being done. His column "Life Over Sixty" appears weekly in *Newsday* on Long Island. It is called "Growing Older" when it is published in more than 475 newspapers around the country. His columns are a fountainhead of information about what is going on in the world of our senior citizens. They are "must reading" for key staff personnel of the House of Representatives Select Committee on Aging, which I have the privilege to chair.

Lou Cottin understands the trauma of people reaching the age of sixty-five and being forced into retirement against their wishes, in many cases without adequate incomes to live on. He knows the problems of Medicare, that many elderly people are caught up in the bureaucratic red tape and are being denied medical services they need because of limiting factors and narrow interpretations of regulations.

He knows, therefore, that Medicare must be broadened to include things such as home health care and homemaker/chore services; that our older people must be provided with eye examinations and eyeglasses, dental examinations, dentures and restorative dental work when necessary. They should also receive, under Medicare, hearing aids, foot care, and annual physical examinations.

There are two recurrent themes in Lou Cottin's columns. "Seniors in the United States are getting a bad deal." The columns named chapter and verse to prove his points. Cottin's writing wasn't just complaints. He was making *demands*. He spread the thought: "We want back in on life—all the way. We are not second-class citizens."

His second theme is even more direct. It runs like this. "Nothing is too good for older Americans. The country owes us. We're the people who fought and won two world wars. People our age beat the depression of the thirties. Our age group developed most of the science and technology which established our present American standard of living.

"Today's lovely homes, factories, offices and improved services come from the work we, who are now old, did. You have computers? *We* introduced and built them. You have better roads and cars? We built them, too. You have medical and other specialists in every field of endeavor? They were our contributions to the country and the world."

That is the theme spelled out in detail in chapter after interesting chapter of this book. It is an angry book by an angry man, almost as old as I am. *Elders in Rebellion* carries forward the work of my Committee on Aging.

What we have been able to accomplish in Congress during the year 1978 alone is due in no small measure to the revolution in how people are thinking about the elderly, a revolution which finds Lou Cottin in the front ranks of the fighters for change.

To name a few of these accomplishments—advances in Home Health Care, congregate housing, passage of a $4.3 billion Older Americans Act extension, wiping out much of the age-based discrimination in retirement practices in the federal government and the private sector, and the anti-crime amendment designating $12 million in federal housing funds for use in improving security and safety in public housing for the elderly.

Bob Weiner, staff director of the House Committee on Aging, told me he believes that Lou Cottin's newspaper columns helped create a favorable climate for the legislation and were a big factor in winning speedy approval of these proposals in the Congress.

Elders in Rebellion is in fact and purpose a message to my Committee on Aging, to Congress, to state and local governments, and to the aged themselves. It says to us, "These are the next steps in our fight for recognition as valid members of American society.

"We, ourselves, must now make this nation value us for our past performance. We, ourselves, must move forward into the mainstream of society boldly, with an eye to future generations of elders."

That's the message of *Elders in Rebellion*. I welcome Lou Cottin to the ranks of fighters in the interests of American elders.

Introduction

We American senior citizens are the most exhaustively analyzed humans in the world. Every phase of our lives has been microscopically examined and dissected for the edification of the American public. All our troubles are fully documented, widely discussed and heavily publicized in all the media of communication.

You can learn about us by attending lectures. You can establish yourself as an expert on "aging" by reading books. You can take college courses in gerontology. You can study the data on aging issued by the Administration on Aging of the U. S. Department of Health, Education and Welfare (especially at election time).

Your county officials, your city fathers, your town or village dignitaries and the heads of all political jurisdictions issue dressed-up statements of how dearly they cherish us older Americans.

You can have the facts on the aged geographically, covering federal, state, city or rural areas. You can learn all there is to know about the economic, health, residential, social, religious and sex problems of the over-sixties.

(Note: Published material on the sex situation among us oldsters is comparatively new. It has finally been admitted that we, too, do what comes naturally. The fact that we don't talk about it so much kept the subject off the front burner until about five years ago. The last four books submitted to me for review were on "sex among the aged." There were no positional diagrams, of course. All these books could be classified as "Right on, you lucky old folks. Sex is OK. More power to you all.")

Yes, it's all in print now. That raises two questions. Why then am I offering another book on the aging? Who am I to write it?

We seniors do not read the books which analyze the problems of seniors. They are written about us, not for us. There is no advocacy in them. The data concern our age group; the mass, not the person. Statistics tell us facts. They don't tell us what to do to change uncomfortable situations.

Victor Hugo said, "The misery of a child is interesting to a mother. The misery of a young man is interesting to a young woman. The misery of an old person is interesting to nobody."

We, of course, know our personal problems. We record each little financial hassle. We describe each little ache or pain. We'll recite our private litanies at the drop of a hat. (If you don't drop a hat, we'll sing our sad song anyhow.) Sure, many of us have become crashing bores. How could we help it? Few of the pundits in the field of aging relate to us as *people*.

Nobody elected me to become a spokesman advocate for

my brother and sister seniors. It's a job I brought on myself. At age sixty-eight, my wife Nikka and I (Nikka was then sixty-seven) faced up to the question of retirement. I'd spent my life working as a moderately successful free-lance business journalist covering business methodology here and abroad. During the last fifteen years at this trade, I was involved in writing about computers and their applications.

Nikka had thirty-four years of elementary school teaching behind her. Our house was paid for. Our two children were successfully on their own. Between Nikka's pension and our Social Security, we thought that we could make it financially in comfort.

We were wrong. Simple arithmetic revealed that our income would be cut in half when we retired. We checked among middle-income people already retired. We discovered that the situation of most middle-income retirees was about the same as ours. For many, however, the percentage of reduction in income due to retirement was greater than ours.

As an older American, I now have a cause that concerns me *personally*. I see that the vast majority of my contemporaries are discriminated against. I face the fact that most of us worked hard all our lives to achieve poverty and an almost total loss of status. I see that the sick and very old among us are tortured in nursing homes. I learn that our years of contributing to growth and joy in our country and in our communities are no longer recognized. I am aware that many of us are scorned even by our own children.

For two years after we decided to retire, I tried to find out how to help my contemporaries. I read all published data I could lay my hands on which related to the aging in this country and abroad. I interviewed gerontologists at several universities. I studied the operations of federal, state and county programs on aging. I checked into the delivery of social services to the aging. I participated in the projects conducted by county Offices of Aging in several states.

So help me, I managed to spend research time at forty senior citizen clubs in the United States. I visited fifteen "Darby and Joan" clubs in England and four in Holland. I also visited many senior clubs in Canada and studied national programs for the aged during a research trip from Montreal to Vancouver.

The result of my studies was cold anger. But anger without action serves no useful purpose. The notes I took listed the facts about the situation of the aged here and abroad.

From facts came ideas for improving unsatisfactory situations and attitudes. I wanted to help change whatever diminishes us seniors as people, or hurts us emotionally, psychologically or physically. My studies abroad showed that every industrial country in the world treats its senior citizens more humanely than does our country.

Late in 1973 and quite by accident, a number of my notes fell into the hands of Lou Schwartz, managing editor of *Newsday,* the Long Island evening paper which reaches more than half a million households daily—a probable readership of 800,000. *Newsday* is the only newspaper in the United States which, every week, devotes a full page called "Life Over Sixty" to the interests of the senior-age population.

A few of my notes were published as columns on the page. The volume of mail from people of all ages was startling. The column is now in its fifth year of continuous weekly publication. National syndication, under the title "Growing Older," began in 1974 through the Newspaper Enterprise Association, the Scripps-Howard editorial service. Latest reports indicate publication in more than 475 newspapers nationally.

It is a good column. It is a useful column. It is a "heads up, let us seniors fight our own battles" column.

It is an urgent call to our beloved adult children. We say, "Look at us, darlings. You will be treated as we're being treated unless you join our fight for a valid, comfortable, useful life after retirement."

However, I have learned that column writing is "potshotting" at issues that concern the aging and those nearing retirement. In 750 words I can cover the highlights of one part of an issue only. Now I need to stop dodging from subject to subject. Now I need to put it all together.

Most of the material in this book comes from discussions with senior citizens. My elderly friends and acquaintances have dictated the order of chapters. Their middle-aged sons and daughters have expressed their fears and expectations about retirement. I have consulted with gerontologists, with public officials and with social service people to ascertain whether the particulars of these experiences are common among the aged and the pre-retired across our country.

With their assistance I've written this book. I've organized the issues on which seniors must fight to achieve a more fruitful life. I present them here as honestly and as completely as I can in the most interesting way I can. I feel that I'm qualified to write this book. I believe the book is needed. I hope readers will agree.

1

Elders: Our Image

There was a time when the word "old" suggested sagacity, kindliness, wisdom, generosity, even graciousness and beauty.

Now, in the United States particularly, the adjective "old" has become an affront. The word leaves an unpleasant taste on the tongue. It is rarely used except with pejorative and accusatory modifiers. We have "old and sick." We have "old and poor." We have "old and doddering, helpless, crabby, crotchety, useless, dependent." Take your choice.

Try this. Tell someone, "You're acting like an old woman." Or say, "You're behaving like an old man." Be ready to duck. But be sure that the person to whom you've addressed the remark is not as big or as strong as you are.

The media are chiefly responsible for making the word "old" a curse rather than a compliment. We can almost feel the glee of reporters as they tell us about nursing home scandals. On our TV screens, we can actually see the zombie-like residents in these and other institutions. For the media, one picture shot in a hospital or nursing home is worth a thousand shots at a sewing circle. Sensation is what sells magazines and newspapers. Drama increases the listening audience of TV stations.

Naturally, it is more exciting to show wretchedness than felicity. A horror picture is more vivid than a depiction of everyday experiences. Suffering is easy to take as long as the reader or viewer is not the one who is suffering. As a result of such broadsides, the public develops a mind-set. "Old" becomes synonymous with ugliness. Aging becomes synonymous with infirmity, misery and dependency.

The TV performances which dissect nursing and adult home operations have the worst effect. We shudder. "Whose breath," we ask with Edwin Markham, "blew out the light within these brains?/Who made them dull to rapture and despair?/Things that grieve not and that never hope?"

As we, the elderly, read the reports and view the broadcasts, each of us is overcome with fear. "Not me!" we cry. "Please God, not me!" We look at our children and wonder. "With all their expressions of love, will they put me away to be warehoused in one of these places? Is this to be my fate?"

We also wonder, "How can such things be, in this, the richest country in the world?" Answers to that question will be offered in other sections of this book.

The media may defend themselves against our criticism that they gloat on our miseries and give us oldsters a bad name. "Be fair," they demand. "Don't we also report the facts about elderly people who performed great deeds in spite of their advanced age? What about Grandma Moses, who painted 'The Rainbow' at age 101?"

Good for Grandma. And let us add a few more "talking

dog" stories which have become standard among the media.

So Carl Sandburg wrote a poem at the age of eighty-five. Frank Lloyd Wright designed the spectacular Guggenheim Museum at the age of seventy-six. Albert Schweitzer won the Nobel Prize at sixty-eight. Winston Churchill was re-elected as Prime Minister of England at the age of seventy-seven. Picasso, in his old age, continued to paint. Rubinstein, at ninety, is still a master at the keyboard.

We are not stupid. A parade of unusually successful old people does not change our image. To be ordinary is not to be *inferior*. The image of commonplace oldsters is not enhanced by extolling the luminaries among us. It's a back-handed compliment.

You and I, brother and sister seniors, have scaled no great heights. Nor are we now in our advanced years setting new stars in the skies or building bridges across great chasms. In this we are like so many millions of seniors who sport no mantles of glory.

Nonetheless, we are worthy of high regard. We must value what we have done in our lives. We need to consider how we may yet enrich our lives and the lives of others in our small ways.

We did not, in our younger days, spend our lives basking in the reflected honor of rare, much publicized personalities. The exceptional ones, even the geniuses among us, could have achieved little without us. The everyday work of the world we know was done by us ordinary, everyday citizens.

Therefore, our image should not, now that we are old, be reckoned by the number of "greats" we have among us. We have our own standards of importance. It is enough that we have shared a lifetime of love with others. It is enough that we served our own little worlds and survived with honor.

Now, we face our private and general trials with courage. We are not to be pictured as non-people. We were not found wanting when we were younger. We are not failures now that we are old.

Throughout our years most of us knew contemporaries who shone with a brighter light than we did. Remember? In kindergarten we had the boy or girl who was able to read at the age of four. Through school we had the brilliant ones who came through with straight "A's" without even cracking a book. In our working years there was always the man or woman marked indelibly for success or fame.

For there we were from our younger days through our middle years. Steadily, firmly, often heroically we carried the burden of the world and the nation. Look, now, what has become of us! At age sixty and older in the United States we, ourselves, have become the burden. Ours is the only industrial nation in the world which, in the main, treats the elderly as charity cases. We are judged by our chronological rather than by our functional age. Even the most efficient among us are driven from our jobs when an arbitrary retirement age is reached.

Our country puts a premium on work for wages or management for profit. The word "man" is recognized. The word "woman" is accepted. In terms of the economy, however, the word "manpower" covers both sexes. When we reach retirement age we are no longer considered as "manpower."

Thus are we diminished. On a certain day at a certain age we are declared and pictured as useless. We are no longer rated in the national manpower statistics. Work gave us status as contributors in society. Now we are not permitted to work. We are treated as suppliants living off the work of others. The subsistence we receive as Social Security is not enough to support us. The financial assistance we receive from Medicare pays less than half of our health and medical costs. The unpleasant image of us as non-producers is thereby extended. We are poor as well as useless. There are none to do us honor.

We are also kept out of sight. In the suburbs and in rural areas, many of us are confined to our homes because we lack adequate bus service. In the cities, the high cost of transportation limits our mobility.

Where we are seen, the quality and content of our social life are determined by young people. As directors of our senior citizen clubs, they decide what our interests and amusements should be. All too often, their concept of our needs is limited to recreational activity suitable for ten-year-olds. Indeed, a contemporary who is a member of one Golden Age club told me that he was called "uncooperative" by his club leader because he refused to play games like Pin the Tail on the Donkey.

There will be no change in our situation until we ourselves fight our way back to a position of importance in this country. In our case, passivity ratifies our status quo. We are, in many areas of our lives, considered to be in second childhood. The speechmakers talk of "dignity" in our old age. Dignity is what we have. Condescension is what we get.

The task of re-establishing the validity of the elderly in this country is difficult. What is called for is determination. We must have faith in our *own* ability to lead the struggle for fundamental changes. The way we are perceived by younger Americans discredits us. The way politicians toss about our basic and general needs demeans us. The way our adult children disregard us ravages us.

We must see ourselves as belligerents in a war for survival as cogent people. "For us to grow old gracefully is to grow old disgracefully." We will need allies. Let's find them, guide them, help them to help us. We will need supporters. Let us be the ones to qualify and quantify the levels of their support.

We, the elderly, know our own problems best. The young and the politicos seem to be seduced by the word "maintenance." They speak of "income maintenance." They refer frequently to "maintenance of comfort in housing for the elderly." And so with health, welfare, recreation, employment, housing, re-education. So, too, with involvement in family and community life.

Maintenance is not enough. Our word must be "improvement." What has been left for us today is not enough, not nearly enough. A tattered image is unacceptable to us. We suffer emotionally, physically and economically.

Ours must be a call to arms, not to alms. Let us group our forces to cover all sectors in this struggle for a place in society. Where anger is needed let us be angry. Where cleverness is needed let us be clever. Where sacrifice is necessary let us give of ourselves with our hearts high and our minds free.

There is an opportunity for every senior citizen to do his bit for the cause of the aged. We may serve in the ranks. We may win positions of leadership. Let us analyze our difficulties. Let us total our assets. Let us assess the strength of the opposition and move to win back our honor. The very least we can achieve is our own self-respect and a new recognition of our own importance.

2

Elders: Our Status

The battle begins the day after retirement. We must learn to march backward. Hup, two, three, four, right out of life as we knew it before we received our walking papers. We shall take our places at the back of the line along with 22 million second-class American citizens.

We see our friendships fall apart. We watch our income shrink to half what it was before we retired. We must not look too carefully at our clocks. The hands of the clocks are still moving, even though it doesn't seem that way. We can't discard our calendars right away. There are still a few notations on them.

These notations were entered on our calendars *before* we retired. There are people to see. There are bills to pay. There are social obligations to fulfill. These hangovers are what remain in our lives from when we were considered "productive" citizens. We need to check with Social Security. We need to clarify our Medicare status. We need to determine how far our new income will go.

From here on in we won't be making dates very often. In time we won't need a calendar at all. That could be for the rest of our lives. We've arrived at the time when every day is Saturday. Now, we know the months by the signs of the seasons. The leaves fall during October. We'll know November because the stores are advertising turkeys. December is easiest. The Santas are out ringing their bells and ho-ho-hoing at every corner. The holly wreaths are on display. January follows New Year celebrations. Spring brings a "Thank God—I've made it."

All right. We leave the calendar and get down to cases. In the United States, retirement from gainful occupation shoves us into a new relationship with society and with the economy. It's not just a matter of being out of a job. An unemployed American may latch on to an income somewhere.

Now that we're retired and unemployed, idleness and boredom are a personal state of being for all our remaining years. We will not deposit a paycheck *ever* again. If we retired before age sixty-two, we won't even have a Social Security check to endorse until we reach that age.

But let's forget the money for a moment. The designation of our status will be "retiree" for about six months; at most for a year. After that, the dignity and honor which our work gave us disappear. We're "senior citizens," or "golden-ager," or "older Americans," or "old biddies," or "old coots." We're the "somebodies who once worked here."

That's logical. Our youth-oriented country puts a premium on the work ethic. The longer we are out of work, the fewer our opportunities to get back into the work force, the further away we are from what is euphemistically called the "mainstream of life." Working, we were somebody. Retired, we became nobody.

We fought our way up in the world to poverty and dis-association. The economy doesn't need us. Our unions don't need us. Our workmates don't need us. Our part in the big ball game is over. A younger man is covering our position on the job and in life. We're spectators now. Stand out of the way and watch the players from the sidelines.

Sometime during the first half year of retirement, we'll get the urge to drop in at the plant or office to visit the "gang." Why not? We left part of our lives with these people at that place. "Surely," we think, "everyone will be glad to see us."

We discover that the firms for which we worked have changed. New people have moved into the offices. New foremen head up operations of which we were a part. Those we knew are facing new problems. Business does not stand still. Retirees do.

Sure, every old friend will be cordial in a "How're-you-doing?" way. But they won't have time for us. Then we'll remember how indifferent we ourselves were when old-timers came back. Of course, we thought that we were different. We aren't. It's a painful lesson.

During the visit, we'll talk about the little annoyances we weathered when we were on the job. "Is that old S.O.B. Robertson still buggin' you? Have they fixed the toilet on our floor? Boy! Wasn't that a riot when it overflowed a couple of months ago? Anything new? Is Alice still carrying on with you know who? How's the new guy (or gal) on my job making out?"

We're waiting to hear at least one former workmate say, "Nobody could handle the job the way you did. We miss you. The department isn't the same since you left." They may or may not say it. They're still working. We're in the past tense. We don't belong. The phrase "out of sight, out of mind" occurs to us. But we're forced to change it. Now the phrase becomes "out of work, out of memory."

For most of us, one experience of this kind is enough. Others among us are more persistent. We try another visit. All the conversation is about current activities. We're out of it. One of the older men or women may bother to ask, "How are you enjoying your retirement?" We cook up a few lies about how great it is to get up at 10 A.M.

To workers still on a payroll, we may be non-persons going nowhere. But in our hearts we know that we're still solid citizens. Others may think that retirement condemns us to ineffectuality. An increasing number of us, however, refuse to accept the situation thoughtlessly and without protest. Others may see us in the past tense. We know that an interesting, useful life is still possible for us.

The decisions are ours to make, as individuals. Ours alone. We can't expect much help from social workers. They're locked into the word "continuum." They will tell us that aging and retirement are simply a continuation of life under new circumstances. Don't believe them! It's a new world.

Our lives as retirees differ qualitatively from our situations as workers. We're talking about the rest of our lives. We have at least ten hours a day to fill. They must be used in new ways. We have new associations to make. They must be established as the result of our new situations as non-workers. There are new unrehearsed and unfamiliar roles to play. How shall we find them?

Take it from the top. There are choices to consider. We can drift aimlessly into retirement. It's just something which happened to us. We became blips in the Social Security computers and in the population statistics. We influence nobody. We help nobody. We hurt nobody. We challenge nobody. We are alone. We *are* nobody.

We can, however, arrange things so that we play games or amuse ourselves for the rest of our lives. It's golf or cards. It's social dancing, or (when we can afford it) social drinking or partying. Here we do, indeed, have human relationships. But the contacts are usually limited to other retirees. To them and with them we can complain, "Our children really don't pay any attention to us. They expect us to thank them for the privilege of baby-sitting our grandchildren."

Put it all into the punch line of the comedian who complains, "I don't get no respect." We surely want to be respected. But what are we doing to *deserve* respect? Being old isn't enough. Past performance doesn't rate. What we do *now*, old and retired as we are, *that's* what counts.

Retirement is a challenge. It calls for involvement. We must restore our status as useful, interesting people. We must believe that being out of a job is not being out of the world. We may audit courses in schools and colleges to sharpen our minds and expand our intellectual interests. We may even register for courses leading to college degrees. We may try to master a musical instrument.

That's only one suggestion. What we're aiming for is to do *something* which will make others glad we're around. Say it plainly. We want to get involved in action we can brag about. We can join an organization espousing a worthy cause. We can contribute as volunteers. We can tie in with activist seniors pushing for increased Social Security or tax reduction for seniors. We can work our way into the political scene. If the politicos set us to stuffing envelopes, we can insist on being part of their serious deliberations.

There are, indeed, many opportunities to work as volunteers. Schools need us. Hospitals need us. Neighborhood centers need us. In some cases, volunteerism may even produce a little income.

Status is being listened to when we talk. Status is being appreciated for what we do. Status is being respected for our contribution. Status is being admired.

In spite of our age? No. *Because* of our age.

3

Elders: Our Health

The observations about our "image" and our "status" as older Americans are obvious generalizations. They apply to some of us only in part. Others may accept most of the statements as correct. No one needs to buy the whole package as written. The general public may mask our separate personalities under the convenient term "senior citizens." But we see ourselves as individuals. We relate to the world and to contemporaries as individuals.

From this vantage point we can write this book as a joint effort. I chronicle the difficulties shared by the majority of us seniors as you have reported them to me. You, the reader, will determine the degree to which you are personally affected by specific situations. Together we will explore just how we are clobbered *because* of our "status" which is negative; our "image" which is demeaning.

Barring a united effort to affect changes under our leadership, the soon-to-be retired will confront problems similar to our own. We will, therefore, ask them a simple question: "How do you perceive your upcoming retirement?" Their answers will dictate the subjects of our book.

A majority of the pre-retired (over fifty) who answered the question said, "It's all a matter of money. If I have enough income I'll enjoy a happy retirement."

A smaller number said, "As long as we have our health, we'll make it."

A few admitted that they expected to be bored. They hoped to get part-time work, but would "take things as they come."

To us who are already retired, the answers of the "money-minded" make sense. We know how our standards of living have dropped. But even fat-cat retirees with high incomes must live in fear. They know that for the aged to be sick is to be sunk, financially, that is.

This brings the question of medical and health care of the aged front and center as the next chapter in this book.

We live in the richest country in the world. We have more and better-trained physicians than any country in the world. We have more hospitals; more available beds; more medical schools than other nations. We have more specialists in various branches of medicine than other countries.

At this writing, we are the only industrial country in the world which does not have a comprehensive all-protective national health plan. That's the beginning of our struggle.

But even that's too simple. Suppose we get a national health plan as described. Will we be out of the woods free and clear? Will we get the medical attention we need? Will the sick in nursing homes be treated for their specific illnesses instead of being doped up and sedated? There are some very unpleasant facts to face.

Check this statement. "Doctors do not like to have old people as patients. A large percentage of the aging are denied access to the technical competence of physicians."

I can hear the murmurs of disagreement. "Where do you come off making a statement like that?" Believe me, brother and sister seniors, I didn't make this up.

Judge for yourself from the summaries of the following official reports. The Gerontological Society of the United States presented the basic case at a meeting run under the title "Seniors vs. the Medical Profession."

The U. S. Senate Special Sub-Committee on Aging also held a public hearing on this question (of doctors and the aged). The title of their deliberations was "Medicine and the Aging: An Assessment of Opportunities and Neglect."

Senator Charles H. Percy (R. Ill.), who is chairman of the Senate sub-committee, presided at the Gerontological Society gathering. He summed up the medical status of seniors succinctly when he said:

"I have solid evidence. There is a lack of concern and knowledge by large segments of the medical community in regard to the illnesses and chronic disabilities which so often accompany aging.

"My sub-committee," continued Senator Percy, "issued a special report about the relative absence of doctors specializing in areas of aging even in nursing homes.

"That report argues that this problem begins in medical schools. Physicians of the future are trained primarily to deal with the medical problems of *young* people. Many physicians *avoid* dealing with the elderly, especially nursing home patients. Many doctors have testified before our sub-committee that *given the demands on their time, they elect*

*to take care of the younger people who can return as pro-
ductive members of society.*"

The psychological reinforcement that comes to physicians
from seeing the sick *cured* is not thought to be available in
the context of the infirm elderly. In his study of nursing
homes, Senator Percy reports, "One doctor told us candidly
—'I hate nursing homes. I never go there. I get too depressed. I never feel like I am doing any good for anyone.'

"Our committee," says Percy, "took exception to this notion. We pointed out that dramatic improvement and often
full recovery are possible even with the most infirm nursing
home patients. Sometimes the remedy is as simple as *taking
the patients off all the drugs they have been receiving.*"

We grant that Senator Percy's hearing was all a plus for
us seniors. But when Senator Percy queried 164 schools of
medicine he asked three questions:

> Do you have geriatrics as a specialty in your curricu-
> lum?

> Do you have programs in which students, interns or res-
> idents serve in nursing homes?

> Do you have programs which help serve nursing homes
> in some other way?

Senator Percy reports, "I received eighty-seven replies to
my questionnaire. Three schools of medicine indicated they
had established geriatrics as a specialty in their curricula.
Seven schools were viewed by the staff as 'very close to this
goal.'"

Given these data, the medical future seems very dim for
us who are already old. It may, in time, be brighter for our
middlescent sons and daughters. But we doubt it. The

movement toward *separating and treating age-related* diseases from other illnesses is not going forward.

Senator Percy concludes, "I, for one, think that the medical profession should extend its blessings to all persons in all age groups, in full understanding of the needs of individuals in each group."

Let us say "Amen" to Senator Percy's comments. Where do we go from there? So little, so very little is being done toward achieving the blessing of specialized medical expertise for us older Americans! What we're up against is the doctor who says, "You're doing all right for a person your age." Or, more gently, "You've got to expect things like this. Remember, you're no spring chicken. Ha, ha."

Nuts to him! We shouldn't be treated for our age. When we go to our doctors we expect them to treat our illnesses, not our age! Cortication of a left leg is an age-related disease. A stomach disorder can happen to anybody.

Let's look at the picture realistically. During our lifetime, medical science developed many specialties. When our wives became pregnant, they consulted an obstetrician. When our children were born we took them to pediatricians. Indeed, medical specialists served us throughout our lives. Ophthalmologists for eye conditions, audiologists for hearing problems, proctologists for rear-end situations, cardiologists for heart conditions, urologists for our prostate troubles.

The medical specialty for age-related illnesses is called geriatrics. For all 25 million elderly in the United States, there are fewer than one thousand geriatric specialists. The magazine *Geriatrics* sets the figure as between five and six hundred.

In our country, moreover, the medical profession does not *recognize* geriatrics as a specialty.

How then do we have a regularly published professional magazine called *Geriatrics* and an active American Geriatrics Society? How, in fact, can we speak of one thousand or six hundred doctors as geriatricians? The answer is that they are all *self-styled* geriatricians. They have chosen this field of medicine as their life work.

They have become members of the American Geriatrics Society, which published the magazine *Geriatrics* in order to spread geriatric education among physicians who are now in *general practice*.

Dr. William Reichel of Franklin Square Hospital, Baltimore, Maryland, has been, for five years, chairman of the Research and Education Committee of the American Geriatrics Society. The Society conducts national conferences on geriatric education. It works with pharmaceutical firms to develop and to conduct educational conferences on geriatric chemotherapy. It designs and provides curricula on geriatrics for medical schools.

Sandoz Pharmaceutical of Hanover, New Jersey, also conducted national meetings for doctors. They covered the subject "Solving the Communication Problem with Older Patients."

The title of that symposium is the tip-off so far as we elders are concerned. Our generation has grown up in awe of our doctors. They tell us very little about the nature of our particular illnesses. My contemporaries tell me that what they get from their physicians is a prescription, orders not to be upset and a bill. And this has been my own experience whenever I failed to ask the right questions.

We respect our doctors. But in many cases the more our

infirmities are "age-related," the fewer the explanations they give us. Some of us consider this a put-down. Our doctors are unfair when they fail to define causes of a specific condition. They do us an injustice when they fail to explain the "why" of the present illness, how it may develop.

We have a right, therefore, to ask our doctors, "When was the last time you attended a geriatrics symposium or seminar?" Merely reminding them that geriatrics is something we have been reading about will be helpful. It may trigger a change in our doctors' attitudes.

There is substantial agreement on one point in the medical profession. Geriatric personnel and nursing home medical care for the aging need considerable improvement. The doctors themselves are of two minds about how this improvement can be achieved.

The American Geriatrics Society is not basically concerned with *qualifying* geriatrics as a specialty like obstetrics or pediatrics. It works in an organized way to prepare *all* physicians for the delivery of effective medical treatment to the aged. And that's what we oldsters care about too.

The New York *Times*, for example, reported recently, "New York Hospital, Cornell Medical Center, has announced the establishment of a professorship in geriatrics." A hospital spokesman said it was believed to be the *"first such chair specifically endowed for the illnesses and disabilities of the aged."*

Let's hope this is the beginning of a new trend in "teaching" hospitals. Let's hope the manufacturers of the medications we take continue working for us. The Roerig Division of Pfizer Pharmaceuticals presented symposia in fourteen cities on the subject "The Socio-Medical Management of the Geriatric Patient." Hundreds of family physicians attended. At the New York symposium (which I attended) more than nine hundred doctors, nurses and members of hospital staffs participated.

Geriatricians like Dr. Leslie Libow, of the Jewish Institute for Geriatric Care on Long Island, see the task differently. He was instrumental in shaping the country's first geriatric medicine training program for staff physicians in hospitals. He believes that with the expected increase in the aging population, geriatrics should be recognized by the American Medical Association as a medical specialty.

The disagreement (if it may be called that) will not be solved in what's left of our lifetimes as aging Americans. Our priorities relate to our own family physicians. We must find the courage to challenge them. We must, indeed, ask them, "When was the last time you attended a geriatric medical conference or demonstration, or a series of lectures on the subject?"

The really ominous situation is one wherein inimical *social* theories endanger our lives. Referring to what he called "condescension medicine" Lawrence Galton, noted medical editor and writer, cites an example. In his book *Don't Give Up on an Aging Parent* (Crown Publishers, N.Y.) he reports, "A British medical officer created a furor in England and in the United States when he declared his belief that 'to treat people over the age of sixty-five is a *waste of medical resources.*' He was, he announced, 'all for automatically labelling "Let Die" any aging person entering a hospital.'"

This gets us seniors back to our own family physicians. The outlandish statement just quoted is certainly extreme. But on a scale of one to one hundred, each of us must rate his or her *own* doctor. Each of us must find out *to what degree* our own doctor subscribes to this "let 'em die" obscenity. If he accepts the dictum in *any degree at all*, get a new doctor at once.

There's a story going around in the medical profession that goes like this:

An elderly patient visited his doctor. "My right knee," he complained, "hurts all the time, Doc. Can you do something to help me?"

Doctor: "Let's take a look at the knee. Take your pants off and get up on the table."

The patient obeyed. The doctor examined the knee. "At your age, Joe, you've got to expect things like this. You're not as young as you were, you know."

"But Doctor, explain something to me. My left knee is just as old as my right knee but it doesn't hurt at all!"

Should you laugh at this joke? Or should you worry?

4

First Interlude

Divorce, in our generation, was neither as easy nor as common as it is today. To us, the phrase "until death do us part" meant exactly that. As the young put it, "We hung in there."

Among the elderly couples we know are people who, to this day, sense each other's moods. They don't need to exchange more than a few apt phrases to understand one another. We also know couples whose conversations rarely get beyond the level of "What's for supper?" There are also the "talking together" couples. They discuss everything they think, hear, see, read or experience.

Nikka and I have been married forty-nine years. We are avid verbalizers. We agreed after days of talk that the writing of this book was a valid project. The conflict developed when I proposed the title "An Angry Old Man."

"Not fair," Nikka protested. "That's a lazy title."

"How do you mean lazy?"

"You'll be writing your book as a personal record of your

private set of angers. That's what's lazy about it. The way our life goes you don't have anything about which to be angry. Under that title the book can be, at best, a clever fraud."

"Do you think my columns are fakeries, too?" I asked.

"You know I don't. If you write your book the way you do your columns, it will be an honest job."

I was mollified. "OK, Nikka, maybe we can be a little more explicit. In writing my column I get around talking to and visiting with seniors who want to turn things over in our favor. I meet with the ones who refuse to take old age lying down."

"Right," she beamed. "You deal with elderly rebels. You understand why they're rebellious; what they're rebelling against. You sponsor their cause. Call the book 'Elders in Rebellion.'"

The name is on the cover. What the name doesn't explain are the difficulties which came up as I ran my tapes at meetings and in private interviews with presumably rebellious seniors.

Getting about among people who believe that they're ill-treated was not a joyous pastime. The problem was to separate personal gripes from the more general difficulties shared by many. A person asking for complaints gets a copious earful. He also gets into arguments.

Among the over-seventy oldsters, one particular misery came up quite often. That related to the increasing alienation of old people from their middlescent sons and daughters.

"All right," said one lovely old spokeswoman. "We understand that our grown-up children are busy. But now the grandchildren are a little bit older too. They don't come

around either. They don't even call us up. It's like we're
dead already!"

The first few times I heard this sorrowful plaint, I com-
miserated with the complainers. I joined the groups in their
head-shaking tsk, tsks. But I finally took my courage in hand.
Wherever the subject came up I hit back.

"Tell me something. What do *you* do to make a visit with
your children interesting and pleasant for *them?*"

It's no fun to be marked lousy by my own contemporaries.
They reacted to the question as though I had defended
Adolf Hitler. Of thirty older Americans with varied backgrounds, twenty-six insisted that they deserved special attention just *because* they were old.

The arguments which developed were acrimonious. These
people really believed that "We gave everything we had for
our children. Now we are entitled to be honored, cherished,
respected, and loved."

My disagreement with this position is total. We seniors
deserve no special consideration unless we earn it by what
we do for ourselves and for others *now*. Yes, we exclude the
sick, the disabled and the doddering. They, of course,
should have the help they need. But we must play our part
in providing such help. Society doesn't pay off on past performances.

Our contributions in the past are not currency for the present. They carry even less weight for our future. If we accept ourselves as "write-offs," we can't blame our children
or society for writing us off.

We cannot expect our middle-aged sons and daughters to
assume a stance of eternal gratitude because we struggled to
raise them. Even less can we expect our grandchildren to

admire us because we baby-sat them and bought them ice cream cones.

Clearly, we who are now old did great things for the world. Surely we served selflessly, giving our best selves to our contemporaries and to our intimates. In all justice, should we not, at last, be permitted to lay down our tools? Isn't it time for us to redesign our dreams? We certainly paid our dues, didn't we? Hell, we're tired!

Yes, many of us are tired. Yes, many of us no longer dream. And yes, many of us are bored beyond bearing. We're rated zero on the usefulness scale. Nobody needs to pay us any attention. Anything that's done for us is done reluctantly and minimally.

Here's a conversation with a congressman who had made his standard speech to an audience of seniors. He played up the "dignity" theme. All the fulsome phrases that follow the vague word "dignity" were included in his oration.

Said the congressman to me, "Good speech, wasn't it?"

"All this jive about dignity, Congressman, just what do you mean by it?" I asked.

He answered testily, "What else is there to say about you old folks?"

"How about telling us what Congress is doing about the problems with which we old folks are wrestling?" I asked.

The congressman thought awhile. "How about you old folks organizing yourselves politically?" he countered. "You claim certain rights for the aged. Don't be vague about these rights. Spell them out. Make a noise. Force me to produce for you."

"Congressman," I asked, "will you then stop talking about our 'dignity'?"

"Darn right I will. And so will other congressmen. We'll

be too busy trying to explain our votes on the bills *you force* us to put into the hopper."

There you have it, brother and sister seniors. The job of improving the conditions of our lives is ours to do. Nothing moves unless we push. Our legislators can't help us. Our children won't help us. Those of us who are active in the fight for our age groups are not special people. We're tired, too. We lose a few. We win a few. But for the most part, we enjoy the involvement.

Abraham Lincoln said, "The wood you chop yourself warms you twice."

So ends the interlude. Let's get on with the work.

5

Elders and Gerontologists

You know now how the word "rebellion" wangled its way into the title of this book. You may have the notion that it's just a quick hop-skip-and-jump from the word "rebellion" to the dangerous word "revolution." Not to worry. We elderly don't want to change the government system. We don't contemplate a fight to change the world. All we elderly rebels want to do is to improve adverse conditions.

Actually, we all need to work our way up to becoming "rebels." Like everything else it's a growth process. It's not something we can jump into. It develops in stages.

Here's a recurrent experience many of us have shared. We'll describe it to define the stages leading to admission into the ranks of elderly rebels.

Your daughter or daughter-in-law phones. The conversation goes something like this: "Hi, Mom, how goes everything in your neck of the woods? Dad OK? Anything new?"

All very pleasant, right? You haven't had a "how're ya doing?" call for several weeks. Count your blessings.

You start to answer the question. "Well, Dad's been having a little trouble with his back. Otherwise we're OK. Nothing new. What's with the kids?"

"That's why I called you, Mom. You know there's a long weekend coming up. We'd like to get away for a trip. Will you mind the kids while we're away?"

Now let's stop right here. We'll interpret this conversation. Suppose you ask, "When will you bring them?" The question implies immediate and unquestioned acceptance of the job.

Note: You haven't asked your daughter, "Why such short notice?" You haven't asked your husband, "Do you want the grandchildren underfoot for three days?" You haven't considered how worn out you both were the last time the grandchildren were parked on your doorstep. You didn't even remember your daughter's criticism when she picked them up, saying, "You spoiled them rotten. I won't be able to manage them for a month. What you don't know about raising kids would fill a book."

Will you accept the statement that in this exchange you acted the perfect patsy? There was no rebellion in you.

Same setup, another view. The daughter asks you to take the kids for three days.

This time you put up a struggle. "Well, I'll have to ask Dad. We do have things to do over the weekend. I'll call you back."

"Aw, Mom. You're turning out to be an unnatural grandmother. Don't you like your grandchildren?"

"Like I said, I'll call you back." Click.

Now, stay with me. How does this exchange affect your rating on the elderly rebel scale? You discuss the matter with your husband. He does not want his weekend cluttered up with the kids. In this case, you've put up resistance. But you have not been a "rebel."

Third example: Same situation. Daughter says, "Take the kids." You say, kindly but firmly, "Sorry, dear. We have plans this weekend."

The daughter pleads, cajoles, begs. She may think, or even say, "What kind of plans can you old people have more important than minding your grandchildren?"

But you, loving grandparents that you are, remain firm. In this small incident you succeeded in putting your own interests before those of your daughter. This makes you a rebel in good standing.

Now, let's study these three unimportant incidents. None are big deals. They happen all the time. We everyday grandparents take them in stride. We do what we think is right. But gerontologists interpret situations of this kind in terms of the relationships of the aged with their children. From these and other small happenings, gerontologists draw general and specific conclusions about the way we seniors relate to younger people.

Gerontology is the study of the aged. It is a discipline which ranges widely among many traditional areas of social life. Literally, as taught in colleges and universities, the meaning of the word is "the logic of aging." It brings together in one group of interdisciplinary courses the many areas of interest related to the elderly.

We seniors have a very important part to play in concretizing the theoretical values of gerontological thought. Let's get to understand the subject and see what we can add to the value *to us* of gerontology as an educational discipline. In his book *The Social Forces in Later Life,* Robert C.

Atchley, of the Scripps Foundation Gerontology Center at Miami University, writes:

> *There are four related but separate aspects to the study of aging (gerontology).*
>
> The *biological aspect* deals with physical aging—the body's gradual loss of the ability to renew itself.
>
> The *psychological aspect* deals with the sensory processes. These include the perceptions, motor skills, intelligence, problem-solving ability, understanding, learning processes, drives, and emotions of the aging individual.
>
> Biological and psychological changes occur with advancing age. They are coupled with the social environment of the individual to produce a third aspect.
>
> The *behavioral.* This aspect of aging deals with the aged person's attitudes, expectancies, motives, self-image, social roles, personality, and psychological adjustment to aging.
>
> Finally, the *sociological aspect* of aging deals with the society in which aging occurs; the influence this society has on aging individuals, the influence they have on society.

Atchley, quoting Clark Tibbits, one of the founders of social gerontology, describes gerontology as "concerned with the developmental and group behavior of older adults. It is also concerned with the social phenomena which give rise to (and arise out of) the presence of older people in the population. Biological and psychological aspects of aging interest the social gerontologist only insofar as they influence the *ways in which the older individual and society adapt to each other."*

That's pretty heavy reading. We need to simplify the scholarly presentation. It must be interpreted in terms of our lives as senior citizens. Let's go back, therefore, to the three mother-daughter situations which started this chapter. We'll assume that we're in a class at college taking gerontology.

The professor is a man of forty. Our class members range in age from nineteen to thirty. Says the professor, "Three grandmothers have responded in three ways to a request to baby-sit the grandchildren for a weekend. What broad gerontological interpretations are possible? Do their experiences relate, for example, to the biological aspects of aging?"

One student raises his hand tentatively. "Could we say that the couple who resisted taking the kids were concerned with the physical wear and tear of caring for the children over a weekend?"

A second student interjects. "It's not really a biological matter. It's psychological. The emotions come into play. *All* grandparents are crazy about their grandchildren. The first couple is typical. They were *glad* to take the kids, no questions asked."

"Then how do you explain the third grandparent couple who said a flat 'no' to baby-sitting their grandchildren?" asked another student. "In my opinion, they're not typical. From a behavioral and sociological standpoint in our society, grandparents consider caring for grandchildren their most important societal role."

The class discussion wanders on until the fifty-minute period is over. The students come to no serious conclusion.

When exam time comes, the questions to be answered will be as general, as vague, as theoretical as the discussions in class.

Many students of gerontology are taking the courses as postgraduates. They know that the discipline is a must for success in all areas of social work. Whatever their specialty, they will find a need for knowledge about the aging.

If they're working with children they will need to understand the grandparents. And so with every age group in all social service relationships.

When an educational institution offers courses in gerontology, we seniors should be invited to participate. Perhaps invited is the wrong word. Inducements should be offered to seniors. Transportation should be arranged. Enrollment should be free. Where the elderly need stipends they should be forthcoming. The rule must be, "No class in gerontology should be conducted without several articulate elderly citizens front and center in classroom discussion."

This is no idle proposal. It serves our purposes as senior activists. It provides an opportunity to get out from under the sociological microscopes. How tired we are of being studied in the abstract! Who knows better than we, the elderly, what the difficulties of aging are? Who can explain better than we how the difficulties developed and what the rewards of aging should be?

The proposal to induce seniors to join gerontology classes also benefits the students. Wherever senior citizens have audited or registered for gerontology courses, the results have been valuable.

Professor Elaine Jacks, Director of Programs on Aging at Adelphi University in Garden City, New York, reports:

"Older persons have enrolled in a variety of our gerontological workshops and courses. Not only have they gained new insight for themselves. They have contributed positively to the value of our courses both for our faculty and for younger students.

"Through their questions and discussions they reinforce and influence the scope and content of the theory and concepts presented. They assure direct interaction among students of all ages. They create a human laboratory. Everyone achieves, at first hand, a sense of the validity of older persons."

Now, the surprise. No activist senior needs to wonder, "Where can I join a class in gerontology?" The Administration on Aging issued a grant to the Association for Gerontology in Higher Education. This is a national organization of more than fifty colleges and universities with headquarters in Washington, D.C. In 1976 the Association issued the *National Directory of Educational Programs in Gerontology*. This massive 1,650-page book tells you where and how to find gerontology "programs." It was prepared for the use of educators, professionals and students. It gives in detail the nature and location of gerontology-related courses, degree programs, educational services and training programs.

Listings are by states. Wherever an institution in any state offers a degree or certificate in an identifiable gerontological component, the details are described. These may include gerontology, geriatrics, aging, older adults, senior citizens, research service on training courses. (The book is Stock No. 017-062-00105-7, Superintendent of Documents, U. S. Printing Office, Washington, D.C. 20402.)

At this point, we seniors need to get back to basics. If we think of ourselves as senior activists or "rebels" we must as-

sume responsibilities that relate specifically to the gerontological educational structure.

We consider ourselves a segregated minority. We seek
changes in the national and local programs which affect our
lives. We rail against those who see services for the aged as
a form of largesse. But we know that there will be no
changes unless we force the issue.

Gerontologists guide the thinking and planning for a majority of the professionals who hold our quality of life in
their hands. Certainly these professionals mean well. But
kind hearts do not necessarily develop good programs.

Our initiative, therefore, must be to conduct a struggle
right from the top. Our experiences, our resentments, our
qualities as cogent older Americans can work for us. We
must study gerontology. We must teach gerontology. There
must be an end to the false notion that the young know
more about the aging than the aging know about themselves.

Into the gerontology classrooms, brother and sister seniors! Learn and teach. Debate and defend. Clear our own
minds of casually accepted clichés about the aged. Clarify
our position as valid people among the gerontologists who
teach or study the aged as abstractions.

Thousands of professors in hundreds of educational institutions will welcome us. If we do this job right, we who are
now old may live more joyously for our remaining years.
And those who will join our ranks as seniors will definitely
enter the company of older Americans with hopeful hearts.

There's no choice here. Do we devote the last years of our
lives usefully? Or do we waste the last years of our lives
playing games?

6

Elders: All in One Box

There goes a "senior citizen." No, wait a minute. A man? A woman? Senior to whom?

There goes a "golden-ager." Strike that. The gold is tarnished. It could be brass.

Try "older American." That's safe enough. But again, the question. Older than whom or what?

Settle on "elders." That at least presumes a level of dignity.

But none of these appellations describes individual persons. We don't know their sex. We don't know anything at all about their backgrounds, their education, their economic status, their former occupation.

Think of it this way. A man states his occupation as a bricklayer. So long as he continues to lay bricks, he remains a bricklayer. Retire him. He becomes a senior citizen. He has lost the special quality, the particular honor his trade gave him.

Apply the same thinking to doctors or to other professionals. They retire. They, too, lose the distinction with which their profession endowed them. Senior citizens, golden-agers or elders are men and women who were once somebodies. In retirement they become nobodies. All retirees had a past.

There is a basic assumption that our concepts, our experiences, our interests merge after age sixty or sixty-five. There are no variants in our lives after retirement. In the entire time span of aging, there are neither "ups" nor "downs." Our activities, our ideas, our hopes have no special meaning. That's how American society views us. Between age sixty-five and ninety, we are leveled off. We are all placed in one box. We are packaged by the experts under the general term "aging," or "the aged."

Of late, gerontologists have begun to differentiate among us. They use terms like the young-old, the mid-old, the old. But these distinctions have not yet been picked up by most of the people involved with service.

The word "aging" is meaningless for any practical purpose. Geriatricians treat the "aging" medically. Both houses of Congress set up committees on aging. States, cities, towns or villages have departments or offices for the aging. From all of this, we get what are called "programs for the aging."

We start aging the minute we're born. An infant five days old has aged five days. The sequence of life runs in specific age-measured cadences. From infant to baby. From baby to boy or girl. From pre-teen to the teens. From the teens to adolescence. And so to the succeeding life changes, all of which are based on age.

For the vast majority of Americans important life changes are cyclic. Events have taken place in five-year or ten-year cycles. A boy of twelve confronts his world with actions and interests altogether different from those of a seventeen- or eighteen-year-old. The twelve-year-old boy is still playing marbles. A seventeen-year-old discovers girls. A girl during those years becomes a woman.

The tendency these days is to marvel at wonders. We gloat about the advances in science, in medicine. We cheer the availability of practical products which make our lives easier. We date our perceptions of changes back three decades or four decades, even five decades ago. We do not ask about age except in terms of what people do.

But there was life in our country long before the twenties. There are elders alive who were children in those years. They are now somewhere between seventy and eighty-five years old. They have a story to tell. We alone can explore what our lives were like in the early years of this century.

We're talking about the years between 1905 and 1930. In those years, many "help wanted" ads read, "Must have diploma." They meant a *grammar* school diploma. The assumption was that very few workers went on to high school. For most of us our education was finished when we'd learned to read, to write, to add and subtract.

The machinery of production became more sophisticated. The want ads changed. Now there was need for a high school education. The ads concluded, "Must have a high school diploma." Want ads today call for college degrees, plus.

A majority of us Americans now over age seventy and those who have arrived at age eighty were virtually without formal education. Older women, particularly, were sketchily educated. Their role in life was to be housekeepers for their husbands and homemakers.

This does not mean that men and women elders in those age groups are not intelligent and aware. Life itself has seen to their schooling. But society continues to refer to the aging en masse, as though we were all the same. The chronological difference between sixty and eighty doesn't count. Our cultural differences are rarely considered.

The over-seventies of today worked a ten-hour day or longer, six days a week. The half-day work on Saturdays was not introduced even for white-collar workers until somewhere in the twenties. The battles for the eight-hour day were not won until the 1930s. We still remember the owner of a steel mill in Gary, Indiana, who said, "If the eight-hour day comes in, I'll close my plant."

We can say truthfully that our trade union victories changed the quality of our lives. There was time for leisure. The middle-income white-collar class had some practice in the use of leisure. A majority of the working class, now in their seventies or eighties, never really learned how to use their free time pleasantly or productively. Women were too worn out by housework and child raising. Men were beaten down by the heavy work they did during those early years in the factories, mines and mills.

Moreover, at that time, the spread in income between blue-collar and white-collar workers was significant. There was a sharp distinction and considerable animus between the two classes. Those who wore ties and came to work at 8:30 A.M. were upper class. Men who wore overalls and answered the factory whistle at 7:30 A.M. or 8 A.M. were lower class. So, too, there were differences in social and cultural interests.

Time passed. The spread between incomes narrowed. It wasn't until the end of World War II that the incomes of industrial workers in our age group caught up with wage levels of white-collar workers. By then, we were in our fifties.

We made more money. We could buy cars. And did. We could invest in homes. We did that, too. We could pay for higher education for our children.

There were two things we couldn't do. There was no way for us to make up for the formal education we had missed. There was no way for us to restore our health. The industrial system and the ten-hour days had drained our physical vitality. By the time we reached our seventies and eighties, many of us were poor, sick and by today's standards illiterate.

During World War II, President Roosevelt froze prices and wages. Unemployed workers received pension plans instead of wage increases. Non-union workers did not. White-collar people at that time were largely non-union.

When we, ourselves, were young, our parents cared for our aging grandparents. They lived with us. Very few of us can remember childhood without a grandfather, grandmother or both sharing the house with our parents.

What we have today is called "independent" old age. It's the "nuclear" rather than the "extended" family. For the elderly today, it is, in fact, loneliness and disassociation from the mainstream of life.

Enter the senior citizen club directors. They're young. They're idealistic. They are absolutely sure they know what we need. "Lady Bountifuls" all of them. Well-meaning people.

Keeping us "busy" for several hours a week is their goal.

We play games. We sew. We shmear on canvas or paper. They condescendingly pat us on our gray heads, saying, "You're just a sweet old dear." There is no effort to help us express ourselves. Discussion, even about age-related current events, is either elementary or non-existent.

That is why only a few of our older men join the clubs. They have been out in the working world. They want and need more than the senior clubs give them. Educated elders can find little sustenance in the child's play programs.

Essentially, most senior club directors never really see us as valid people. They treat us as though we are children. They perceive us as people with no interests except to stay alive. Local or world problems, they think, are not for us. In this way, they confirm the low esteem in which we elders are held.

Younger elders, mostly retirees in their sixties, stay away from senior clubs in droves. They demand more than "busywork." They want programs with substantive content. They look for lectures, for challenging ideas, for discussion groups on varied subjects.

Aware of this, county offices of the aging have set up multi-purpose senior centers. These, definitely, were giant steps forward in the range of services to the aged. The multi-purpose centers could accommodate seniors of all ages and every interest. Cities and the counties hired professionals in the field of the aged to direct these centers.

Over the country right now, the number of multi-purpose centers is comparatively small. Statistics vary. But for the 22 million elderly in the United States, the accepted number of multi-purpose centers is approximately five thousand.

The multi-purpose center is an idea whose time has come.

The time must come when there will be a greater number of multi-purpose centers than senior citizen clubs. Every multi-purpose center will have one bus or more to gather up elders of all ages. They will provide opportunities for older Americans sixty and older to learn from each other.

Setting up such centers will be a matter of money. It will also require taking a special yearly census of the aged in every community. Right now, nobody knows where we elders live. No one has classified us by how we manage. Nobody knows whether we're rich, poor, sick, well, hungry or handicapped.

Fortunately, there is a form of census available. It covers the children. Each year this census is used to find out how many children, of what ages, will enter or return to school in September.

In several states, activists among the elders have sponsored a useful proposal. Take the door-to-door school census as required. Add three or four questions about the aged. "Are there persons over sixty-five living here?" "Are they well or ill?" "Do they participate in the senior citizen programs available to them?" If the answer to the third question is "yes," the census taker asks, "How do you enjoy the programs?" You get the idea.

This project has been proposed to the New York State Legislature every year for the past three years. It has always been buried in committee. The offices of aging throughout the state still do not know where or how their elders live.

Well, 1980 is a census year. But it won't be special for elders. The usual questions will be asked of all citizens. Perhaps county computers can separate basic data about elders from data about the young. But once in a four-year census period will not be enough. We will still need to know how to reach elders in time to help them live more safely and more abundantly.

On the basis of such a yearly census of the aged, city, village and county offices of the aging could operate more effectively. They would not, as now, be required to use outworn data or guesswork. Decisions about what to do for the elderly would have more substance.

The key to those decisions would surely lead to the establishment of more multi-purpose centers. Such centers would operate six days a week. They would bring together many of the young and *all the old*. Both groups would benefit.

Most multi-purpose centers are now variously funded. In some areas, school districts carry the financial burden. In others, county and local offices of aging organize and sponsor them with community support. It's a mixed bag that produces mixed concepts of what, whom and how a multi-purpose center should serve.

The difference between a senior citizen club and a multi-purpose senior center is not a matter of numbers only. The clubs are open three afternoons a week. The centers are open from nine to five daily. (Some open on Sunday as well. That's the loneliest day for elders who are single.) The clubs accommodate from twenty to fifty oldsters. The centers serve a larger community. The clubs provide a limited number of programs. The centers offer a full range of programs.

From there on, however, centers and clubs are essentially the same. Both are programmatically basic *put-downs* of the elderly. Both sponsor "busywork." Their programs permit the elderly to do during the day what they did in the evening during their working years. No one *grows* at either a club or a center.

An award-winning multi-purpose senior center reports on

its programs as follows: "Classes in ceramics, painting, crafts, woodworking, sewing, dramatics, yoga, bridge and photography."

More agencies provide on-site services such as "health screenings, tax assistance, consumer advice, education."

What, then, is the gripe? There are no stimulants to the mind. In these centers there are no discussion groups. There are no lectures. There is nothing which recognizes us older Americans as citizens interested in our communities. The programs divorce us from the world. Some of us elders will live long enough to see multi-purpose senior centers which will become true community centers. Advocacy will be encouraged. Politics will be discussed.

Their purposes will expand from so-called leisure time activities (read "busywork"). Age differentials will be recognized. The eighty-year-olds will teach the sixty-year-olds, and vice versa. With the help of the appointed professionals, we will run our own show.

Multi-purpose centers will have advisory committees whose members will represent our different age groups. They will reach down to our middlescent sons and daughters. They will provide programs to entice our teenage grandchildren to join.

They will, indeed, be open from 9 A.M. to 11 P.M. Activities of interest will be available every hour of the day. Younger elders will associate with older elders on equal terms. Youth will join us, not on orders from parents. They will gladly partake of our experience because they respect us—because they love us.

We are what our past has made us. Every one of us needs to find an interested audience with whom we can discuss our life experiences. We need to prove that exchanging pictures of our grandchildren is not the total of our years of living. Our pasts are important to us. We delve into our personal histories. From them, we extract events which relate directly or indirectly to contemporary problems.

Activists among us have, therefore, an important job to do. We must take firm leadership of the campaign to increase the number of multi-purpose senior centers. In such centers throughout the nation, we will grow in stature. Young people and old will listen to our thoughts and discuss them seriously.

The word "wisdom," as applied to the elderly, is thrown about loosely. Politicians use that word because they don't have any other attractive concept to apply to us. Our middlescent sons and daughters rarely use the word. They don't think we're wise at all. They want us to sit in corners and remain quiet. We can't accept this position.

But we all know what we are. We remember what life was like during the wars most of us experienced. We remember the depression and the years of our struggles during those rough times.

Our over-eighties have stories to tell. Our over-sixties have different tales to relate. There are lessons to be learned from what has happened to us. We alone can teach these lessons. That way we become one with the present. That way, also, we can guide the future of our beloved children and grandchildren.

The multi-purpose centers become our outlet. There we can shine. They will not be places where we swap reminiscences. They will be institutions where we learn from each other and teach the young.

Our goal must be several multi-purpose *community* centers in every political jurisdiction depending on population.

In these centers we, the elderly, will guide the professional staff. Under our leadership, they will give the young a chance to recognize us and our qualities as people. In these centers, we elders can learn and teach at the same time.

Further education, as it is called, will become a two-way street. That's what it should be. It calls for a giving and taking of theoretical knowledge confirmed by experience.

Experience? That's what we elders have. Name one group in this country which has more.

7

Elders and Programs

Take it from the top. We go back to the Declaration of Objectives of the Older Americans Act. It says: "Section 101. The Congress hereby finds and declares that, in keeping with the traditional American concept of the inherent dignity of the individual in our democratic society, the older people of our Nation are entitled to, and it is the joint responsibility of the government of the United States and of the several states and their political subdivisions to assist our older people to secure equal opportunity to the full and free enjoyment of the following objectives:

(1) An adequate income in retirement in accordance with the American Standard of Living.

(2) The best possible physical and mental health which science can make available and without regard to economic status.

(3) Suitable housing, independently selected, designed and located with reference to special

needs and available at costs which older citizens can afford.

(4) Full restorative services for those who require institutional care.

(5) Opportunity for employment with no discriminatory personnel practices because of age.

(6) Retirement in health, honor, dignity—after years of contribution to the economy.

(7) Pursuit of meaningful activity within the widest range of civic, cultural and recreational opportunities.

(8) Efficient community services, including access to low-cost transportation, which provide social assistance in a coordinated manner and which are readily available when needed.

(9) Immediate benefit from proven research knowledge which can sustain and improve health and happiness.

(10) Freedom, independence and the free exercise of individual initiative in planning and managing their own lives."

This is a statement of objectives. Nobody says that they can all be accomplished. But why can't we achieve *some* of them? "An adequate income in retirement." "The best possible physical and mental health which science can make available."

We need to examine the *process* by which these desirable objectives are *not* achieved. That way we can determine what to do in order to make them (or some of them) real. It's all too obvious that few of these conditions obtain for the vast majority of us elders. The opposite is unfortunately true.

To begin with, the federal government directs the programs primarily through the Department of Health, Education and Welfare (HEW). There, the Administration on Aging (AoA) has responsibility for the various titled programs and activities which define the terms of the Older Americans Act.

Under this act, the moneys allotted for definite services or types of services to us elders are spelled out. These are titled or subtitled with Roman numerals. Title VII, for example, covers the Nutrition Program, which is supposed to assure every elder one nourishing hot meal a day (if he or she can get to such a center). Title III includes state agency activities, area planning in counties, social services, etc.

Through the AoA, allotments of money (through "block grants" or "revenue sharing") are distributed to state offices of aging. From the state capitals the money is distributed to area agencies, townships, cities, suburban and rural jurisdictions.

The list of services runs through every activity which affects our lives as older Americans. These may include such matters as: employment, volunteerism, education for the elderly, community action, economic assistance, housing, health and mental health, nutrition, transportation, job training, research, supportive and protective services. The list is impressive. But it's not tedious. After all, that's how we *live*, isn't it?

The governor of the state appoints a Director of Senior Affairs, or a head of a Senior Department. The mayor of the city appoints; the town supervisor appoints; the village authorities appoint. Down the line all officials serving seniors are politically *appointed*.

In some states the lower-echelon employees are on civil service. In other states they are not. Where they are on civil service, the lower echelons stay on the job. Where they are not on civil service, theoretically, the entire department may be fired. We see, therefore, that *political* considerations often dominate when a new governor, mayor, county or town supervisor is elected to office.

The Older Americans Act also requires that a body of citizens, usually twenty-five to thirty in number, serve on "advisory councils" for the titled programs in states, counties and area agencies. Here again, the governor of the state, mayor of the city, supervisor of the county appoint the members of the councils.

It is logical to conclude that a majority of the membership of these advisory councils will be active in the political party in power. Or they will be *safe* supporters of the party. Thus, when a maverick, that is, an independent person, becomes a member of an advisory committee, he or she will more than likely be a lonely person crying in the wilderness.

During the three years that I have attended the regular meetings of the Advisory Council (Title III) of Nassau County, New York, I have never successfully challenged or even minutely changed a single policy or program.

Across the board, the advisory councils fulfill the *legal* requirements for their existence. But they are, by design, rubber stamps in purpose and in fact.

In my own county the head of the Department of Senior Citizens' Affairs let it be known, right from the start, that she, and only she, could countermand *any* decision voted by the Council.

Similarly, public hearings are a joke. The law says, "Hold public hearings." Have you ever been to one? The leading politicos of the county are there. They listen to reports, speeches, appeals. They even take notes. But no *debate* is allowed and the net result is frustration.

What we elders need is to take matters into our *own* hands. Otherwise, we're sunk. We are left to the tender mercies of politicians whose basic job is to get elected.

Our national organizations are the American Association of Retired Persons (AARP) and the National Council of Senior Citizens (NCSC). Join either or both of them. Then deal with your city, your county, your township or village.

Somewhere in the United States, every problem of the aged has been *solved*. The trouble is that it's been solved *locally*. The questions are, How can we elders find out about the local services which exist in any area? How do we get the same or equal service *for our own areas?*

We cannot expect our state politicians to concern themselves with our needs. They move only when pushed. Even then, they vote just as their leaders tell them to. A state Republican submits an idea and the Democrats nix it or vice versa. Very little is accomplished.

What we elders need to do is to determine our local priorities for ourselves. We'll cite an example.

There has never been a census of the aged. Our number is not known. The state of our health, the conditions of our lives, our incomes, have not been charted.

We don't know, therefore, how many we are, where we live, with whom we live and how we live.

Yes, a census of the aged has been proposed as *part* of the census which tells how many students will be in school next term. But nothing comes of that either.

Just think of what we could learn from such a census! All the programs offered by the government would be made specific for each older person. Surely, they'd pick up some facts about the lost souls who never heard, for example, of the Nutrition Program. Certainly they'd know at least *where* they lived, how and what they ate.

Right down the line, such a census would serve elders in many ways. The lonely elders would find friends. The elders who are ill would be cared for. The elders who are lost would be found.

Consider an example. Different parts of the country addressed themselves to the question of "Crime Against the Elderly." The Assembly of New York State actually *passed* a bill to distribute $35,000 worth of whistles among us elders. Tweet, tweet—that scares the hoodlums. That is, if we can get the whistles out of our pockets or purses in time. Wisely, the New York State Senate failed to pass the bill.

Both houses in Albany then voted to punish juvenile criminals more harshly. Why not? It wouldn't cost any money. New York's governor realized that you can't sentence juvenile criminals until you *catch* them. He vetoed that bill. Now the elderly in New York State have no protection at all until the next session of the State Legislature.

We don't know what foolish ideas will be proposed in the Legislature. But we are aware that there is, in Levittown, New York, a project which could help us. It is a device which blows sirens. It turns a light on outside the residence. It is delivered *free* to elderly citizens.

If in Levittown, why not elsewhere? Additionally, the installers of the safety device are all elders working under the Comprehensive Employment and Training Act (CETA), Title IX of the Older Americans Act.

From Levittown, we go to Multnomah County, Portland, Oregon. There, a two-year survey produced the facts about criminal victimization of the elderly. The money for the survey ($35,000 for two years) came from the federal Law Enforcement Assistance Administration (LEAA).

In July 1977, with the facts at hand, Dr. Marlene Rifai, Multnomah's Director of Public Safety, launched a positive plan. The twofold purpose of the plan was:

(a) To educate seniors and to train them for self-protection.

(b) To supply and install safeguards in the homes of elderly Oregonians.

The training program produced, in terms of response, greater confidence in the whole criminal justice system. It offered proof that Multnomah *wanted to protect* its senior citizens.

Multnomah County provided $100,000 to make the homes of the elders safe. There was no cost to seniors. Experts, checking back on the data of the survey, installed new burglar-proof locks. They set up alarm systems in homes that needed extra protection. In homes where easy access through windows might tempt intruders, the windows were fixed for safety.

"Seniors who feel safe, snug and secure in their homes," reported Dr. Rifai, "approach each day with confidence. They know they are cherished. They are *psychologically* prepared to participate conscientiously in the safety educational programs we conduct."

A third report comes from Cuyahoga County, Ohio. Here, too, a survey preceded the initiation of a "safety for seniors" project. The staff questionnaire circulated over five areas in the county. Interviewers, who administered the questionnaire, were trained to add details which might reveal special conditions.

The results of the survey revealed that 19 per cent of the respondents had been victims of crimes during the preceding year. In order of their frequency these were: purse snatching, larceny (theft and attempted theft), vandalism, breaking and entering, auto theft and swindles.

Ms. Robinson, Cuyahoga County's Senior Safety and Security Coordinator, commented, "Crime has two elements—intent and opportunity. Our program tries to eliminate the *opportunity*. We can't do much about intent."

The senior protection project in Cuyahoga County was a coordinated effort to educate all seniors. Poverty areas, working-class areas, middle-income and wealthy areas were covered. In 1974, the county commissioners received a grant of $65,000 from the Law Enforcement Assistance Administration. Federal contributions covered a five-year grant of $67,505. The local match for the federal funds was $3,755.

The police helped. Local members of the AARP helped. Volunteers and coordinators helped. Additional help came from the twenty hours a week of paid work of people under Title IX of the Older Americans Act.

The training course covered burglary, intruders, fraud, con artists. Special emphasis was placed on self-protection and self-defense.

What we have here are examples of *local* proposals. The first proposal for a census of the aging could be tested in one county or local jurisdiction. If it revealed substantive information, it could apply in counties, townships and villages. It could also apply to states.

The three proposals cited relate to safety for seniors. The money is available from the federal government through the LEAA. Why haven't areas in other states applied for and received such moneys?

The answer, of course, is politics. The *will* to help us elders is not there. Services to us, the aging, are a hodgepodge of individual local programs and projects.

When a local program succeeds, it should be tried everywhere. There is need for an interchange of basic ideas which would assure that all elders get the same treatment. What is good for one elder could be good for all.

A Senior Speak-Out was held in the city of Albuquerque, New Mexico, several years ago. One thousand elders came to the city's Civic Auditorium. They were there to tell the politicians what was bothering them. This time, the politicians were there *to listen.*

Time segments were allotted to seven topics. These were: health care, transportation, legal and tax problems, financial matters, social services, nutrition, home nursing care.

Elders wishing to speak lined up before numbered "subject" microphones. Those who didn't get a chance to speak submitted their concerns in writing. More than two hundred letters were received.

The Speak-Out called for cooperation among the *independent* organizations of senior citizens. Among other things, as a result of the Speak-Out, seven mini-bus routes were set up. A senior law assistance program was established. Two lawyers worked with four senior advocates. They were assigned to represent the elderly in dealing with landlords and the Veterans, Social Services and Health departments.

Here, *we elders* did the talking. Here, the politicians listened to *us*. Could not such a project be established in varied forms elsewhere?

Our need is to express *ourselves*. The job of elders is to forsake humility. When we speak up, the politicians must listen.

Their *jobs* depend on it.

8

Elders and Nursing Homes

This book is not being written for nursing home patients. Only a few of them will understand. Elders in nursing homes are not rebels.

We say this without reservation. The worst thing that can happen to an older American is to be put away in a nursing home. It is a stage in life we would all like to avoid. Ask yourself, therefore, "What chance is there that *I* will get to the point where I will be 'placed' in a nursing home?"

A widely published study by Dr. Robert Kestenbaum of Wayne State University notes, "While one in twenty seniors is in a nursing home or related facility, on any given *day*, *one out of five of us will spend some time in a nursing home during our lifetimes.*"

There is reason to run scared. Burton Dunlap of the Urban Institute puts it another way. He estimates that 25 per cent of the total aging population (about 4 million people) require some type of care for *chronic* illness.

The breakdown, according to Dunlap, would be as follows: "Nursing Homes 600,000; home health care 1.3 million; congregate living facilities or help in preparing meals 1.1 million."

He concludes, "It appears evident that if 2.4 million elderly in the community do *not* have their needs for home health supportive services met, they will deteriorate to the point where institutionalization will be necessary. Or they will die."

Most patients entering a nursing home will die there. Conservative figures indicate that 50 per cent of nursing home patients die in nursing homes; 21 per cent are returned to hospitals. Only 19 per cent are sent home (or to relatives' homes); and 10 per cent are placed in other accommodations.

Please read these figures again. Apply them to what may be your *own* life in your old age. The 10 per cent who are placed in other accommodations is the tip-off. Where do they go? To other nursing homes? To asylums? To boardinghouses which cater to the aged? To firetraps? To rooming houses where their lives are in danger from fire? Make believe it is happening to you. That way you will understand what follows.

There are sharp increases in the death rate associated with transfer to nursing homes. Elders regard nursing homes with fear and hostility. It has been documented that old people believe that entry into a nursing home is a prelude to death. Substantially higher death rates were recorded, for example, among those *admitted* to nursing homes as compared to those waiting to be admitted.

This phenomenon has been termed "transplantation shock." One researcher recorded a 42 per cent death rate for those *admitted* to institutional facilities; 28 per cent for those waiting for admission.

Ask then, "Is there a nursing home in my future?"

Here is another part of the picture. Ninety-five per cent now living in nursing homes are over sixty-five. Most are female or widows. Most are alone. Most patients come to nursing homes from private homes. Less than half the patients can walk. They take or are given large quantities of drugs and sedatives. Recent studies indicate that an average of seven different drugs is taken two or three times daily. Will *you* get your medicines when you need them? Or will you be sedated?

"Nursing Home Care in the United States, Failure in Public Policy" was the title of the "Introductory Report" prepared by the U. S. Senate Sub-Committee on Long-term Care. The special committee on Aging of the United States Senate published their report December 1974. Keep in mind that phrase "Failure in Public Policy." There were what are called "Supporting Papers." One of them read, "The Litany of Nursing Home Abuses," an examination of the roots of the controversy.

Others were:

"Drugs in Nursing Homes: Misuse, High Costs and Kickbacks."

Supporting Paper No. 3: "Doctors in Nursing Homes: The Shunned Responsibility."

Supporting Paper No. 4: "Nurses in Nursing Homes": the heavy burden—the reliance on untrained and unlicensed personnel.

Supporting Paper No. 5: "The Continuing Chronicle of Nursing Home Fires." There were 4,800 nursing home fires during the four years before 1974. There is reason to believe the number of nursing homes failing to meet fire safety standards is increasing. The 1974 study indicates 72 per cent of U.S. nursing homes have one or more major fire deficiencies.

Supporting Paper No. 6: "What Can Be Done in Nursing Homes: Positive Aspects of Long-term Care." Don't condemn the *entire* nursing home industry. There are some good ones but they are hard to find.

Supporting Paper No. 7: "The Role of Nursing Homes in Caring for Discharged Mental Patients." Charges of "wholesale dumping" of patients have been made in several states. Acute problems have been reported, most notably in California, Illinois and New York.

Supporting Paper No. 8: "Access to Nursing Homes by U.S. Minorities." Only 4 per cent of the 1 million nursing home patients in the United States are members of minority groups. Their health needs are, however, proportionately greater than most.

Supporting Paper No. 9: "Profits and the Nursing Home: Incentives in Favor of Poor Care." A joint study conducted by the General Accounting Office (GAO) suggests significant increases in total assets, revenues and profits for operators of nursing homes.

That was in 1974.

We may presume the conditions are little improved today, but we can't be sure of that either. Congressman Claude Pepper, at least, suggested this when he said on June 8, 1977, "There are lessons to be learned from governmental attempts to curb abuses in nursing homes. Governmental attempts to regulate nursing homes have taught us that over-regulation sacrifices compassionate care to impersonal bureaucracy. Underregulation fosters substandard conditions."

Charles J. Hynes, Special Prosecutor for Nursing Homes, Health and Social Services (New York), has stated that "The delivery of health care services to the sick and infirm elderly is a well-documented failure." (Note how that word "failure" comes back.) "For more than two years my office has been making a frontal assault on the abuses committed by operators of nursing homes.

"With the cooperation of the New York Department of Health, we have made great strides in ridding the industry of the *worst operators*."

There's a two-angled aspect to the Hynes investigation. We accept the fact that money is involved. He expects to recover $70 million. That's from seventy-nine proprietary nursing homes. It represents the audits of 25 per cent of the nursing home beds in the state. The submitted reports have already identified *overstated* costs of $13,303,773.

The kickback schemes fall into three categories:

1. Inflated billing: A supplier gives the nursing home a bill in an amount exceeding the amount owed for goods and services.

2. Phantom billing: In which the supplier would give the nursing home official a complete bill for deliveries never made.

3. "Phantom items": In which the supplier would bill the nursing home official for deliveries which were made. But the bill would also include terms not included in the delivery.

The way this shapes up is peculiar. Prosecutor Hynes, and presumably prosecutors in other states, could only go after the *crooks*. They could levy fines against them. They could send a few of them to jail.

But neither Hynes nor other state prosecutors could punish proprietary nursing home operators for *mistreatment, for abuse or for neglect* of nursing home patients.

Of course, this is only the tip of the iceberg. What we are mostly concerned with is patient care. Levels of care are undermined indirectly when funds committed to such care are diverted to private pockets. They are undermined directly in the way some health facility staff discharge their responsibilities.

Hence, we go to the question of patient abuse. Nursing home patients are literally at the mercy of their environment. It is physical incapacity which planted them there in the first place.

The preservation of the rights of these ailing citizens is the purpose of the Patient Abuse Program. A breakdown of basic housekeeping has all too often characterized nursing home operation.

Traditionally, the population of health care facilities depend on their relatives. But if they have no relatives, too bad! In some cases they call in interested community organizations. In other cases, public bodies help them assert their rights. But it's all catch-as-catch-can!

Teamwork between the Health Department and the Hynes unit is logical. Patient neglect and abuse are endemic to the situation in most nursing homes. The sharing of responsibilities may encourage superficial performance except in obvious cases. A nursing home operator, for example, was convicted of willfully violating the State Hospital Code. He maintained unsafe and unsanitary conditions in his nursing home.

But in other cases, prosecution is either not warranted or not possible. Professional licensing authorities, moreover, are loath to take disciplinary action. They prefer to issue *warnings* rather than license denials. Only in rare cases are licenses actually revoked.

We go back for a brief paragraph to the possibility that one out of five of us will spend some part of our lifetime in a nursing home. It may be you or your wife. What, therefore, concerns us is the *total* picture.

In the first place, *nursing home administrators dominate licensing boards* in many states. This perpetuates abuses which the nursing home licensure program was designed to eliminate.

William H. Hutton, Executive Director of the National Council of Senior Citizens, charged that nursing home operations in twenty-nine states were in a position to dominate state boards. In another thirteen states, administrators could dominate their boards with the assistance of one other board member who might have a financial interest in nursing homes.

The list of abuses in proprietary nursing homes is well documented. What crueler abuse is there, for example, than to have an elderly person confined in a home with no money of his or her own to buy even a package of Life Savers? Yet managements of many nursing homes keep every cent patients receive from the government.

Supplemental Security Income, indeed, does mandate that recipients retain a portion of their allotment for personal needs. In practice, this law has not been implemented. Many proprietors charge residents the total amount of their grant.

A report written by a volunteer states, "What has affected

me most is the atmosphere of lethargy that pervades the entire facility. It engulfs even the outsider who steps across the threshold. The seats in the dim lobby are occupied by lifeless bodies. They do not communicate with each other. Their empty faces, their expressionless eyes mark them as robots. They are old, decrepit human machines who sit all day wrapped in their own little world, waiting, waiting . . . for what? Perhaps the end that will release them from the monotony of their daily existence is death."

The drab, listless physical environment is the rule rather than the exception. Food services in many nursing homes can only be described as abysmal. At a recent hearing to *revoke* a facility's license, one person testified that she observed a kitchen which violated *every* sanitary code. The utensils were thick with grime. Food had been left uncovered. Cockroaches were everywhere. The license, however, was *not* revoked.

One attempt by the Board of Social Welfare to monitor diet was to require periodic weighing of residents. However, operators thwart the law by falsifying weight data.

The problem of daily sustenance—essential to the body as well as an important social function—is compounded by the lack of trained and concerned personnel.

One instance was the subject of a grand jury report. A resident failed to attend meals regularly for about a month. One morning it was discovered that he had died. The cause of death? "Cardiac and respiratory arrest precipitated by malnutrition caused by starvation.

"At the time his body was discovered (on the morning of January 12, 1976) his remains appeared extremely emaciated. The corpse was 5 feet 8 inches at the time of death. He weighed 48 pounds."

This case produced a grand jury report. Please note. It did *not* produce a *prosecution.* In nursing homes neglect, in and of itself, is not subject to *penal sanction.*

Here, according to the American Jewish Congress, are the ten minimum standards for nursing home operation:

1. Occupational therapy
2. Frequency of visits by physicians
3. Regular overview by geriatric specialists
4. Use of drugs
5. Treatment of disoriented patients
6. Emergency services
7. Building safety
8. Frequency of visits by families of patients
9. Quality of food and food service
10. Accommodations that assure comfort

The Institute of Gerontology at the University of Michigan/Wayne State University, expands this ten-point program in a booklet, *How to Choose a Nursing Home* ($1.00). It's worth the money. The introduction to this booklet is interesting. "Today," say the gerontologists, "no public or private agency has devised a comprehensive system to rate nursing homes in Michigan. Since there is no such system it is the responsibility of the individual consumer to make the decisions about selection." Following are some excerpts from the checklist included in this booklet. (Note: 80 per cent of the nursing homes in the state of Michigan are operated privately for profit.)

1. A skilled nursing home should provide comprehensive nursing care under the constant supervision of a *registered* nurse on each shift.

2. Important: Visit, Observe, Listen, Ask, Even Smell!

3. Make your visits to nursing homes without prior appointment. Go several times, at different times during the day, especially during meal hours. Pay particular attention to types of meals served.

4. Did "staff" seem to care for patients as human beings?

5. Were the administrator and nursing director readily available? Were they willing to show you around? Were you able to see *every* part of the home? You should be.

6. Was the *current* year's license from the State Health Department prominently displayed? Does the administrator have more than one home to manage? Who is in charge when the administrator is away?

7. On admission, does the home make an inventory of the patient's possessions? What rules must patients follow? Can patients bring items of personal furniture?

8. Does the home make *extra* charges for services such as feeding a patient? Caring for an incontinent patient? Special diets? Note: Medicaid and Medicare *bar* such charges.

9. Are there special charges for visits by physicians and related services? Are drugs and items such as haircuts and personal laundry charged for? Does the home provide a *written* list of such charges? (Patient or relatives should approve these charges in *advance*.)

10. Are *all* bills itemized including drugs? Are patients

charged for wheelchairs, walkers, crutches and canes? (There shouldn't be when Medicare and Medicaid are involved.)

11. Does the patient know he is entitled to $20 a month for personal expense under Medicaid? Patients who receive Social Security are allowed an additional $7.50 a month for spending allowances for a total of $27.50.

12. Be sure you understand how long Medicare or Blue Cross or Blue Shield or other health insurance will pay for care.

13. Does the home ask for a lifetime contract? Does it include medical care? *Not all do.* (If a lifetime contract is involved, see your lawyer.)

We could go on. But if you're planning to enter a nursing home or to place Grandma in one this booklet is an absolute *must*. It's the biggest dollar's worth in the country for the families of nursing home patients.

The Institute of Gerontology of the University of Michigan/Wayne State University deserves the praise of every American. They've made it possible for all of us to analyze and compare nursing homes. The title again—*How to Choose a Nursing Home*.

May we never be required to live in one. But if we are among the 5 per cent of senior-agers forced to enter one, let's be sure we know where we're going.

There are volunteer services available which make it possible for us to determine whether or not a nursing home is functioning in the interests of patients. The Ombudservice is one. Operation Independence, a project of the National

Council on the Aging (NCOA), is another. Leadership of both organizations is funded by federal and state moneys.

The volunteers working for both groups have what would seem to be a simple assignment. "Visit nursing homes. Check the medical and social services they provide. Act as *advocates* for patients."

But there is no law *in any state* which requires nursing home operators to *admit* volunteers. In many states, therefore, a majority of nursing homes close their doors to these volunteers.

Does this tell us something? Is it safe to say that nursing homes *who refuse admission to ombudsmen* and other patient advocates have something to hide?

Here's a clear case where, as the saying goes, "There ought to be a law."

A congressional hearing in Washington sought to find out:

"To what extent is organized crime involved in Medicare, Medicaid and other federal health care programs? Is organized crime extending this involvement?" The date was October 4, 1978. The convener of the hearing was, as you might guess, Representative Claude Pepper (D. Fla.), chairman of the House Select Committee on Aging. Pepper's staff sent questionnaires to thirty states. Ninety-eight per cent of the replies declared, in effect, that "organized crime is increasingly involved in the rip-offs of government health care programs."

The responding law officials were federal and state enforcement officers and police chiefs. They identified for the committee the areas where they had evidence of organized crime involvement. These areas included the following:

1. Ownership and operation of nursing homes.

2. Operation of pharmacies.

3. Ownership and operation of prepaid health plans.

4. Syndicate ownership of clinical laboratories.

5. Syndicate ownership of medical supply houses that produce durable medical goods.

6. Organized crime involvement in the ownership or operation of hospitals and home health agencies.

Now, back to the hearing. Leading off, we had Attorney General Griffin Bell. He is head of the U. S. Justice Department. Bell declared, in part, "There is insufficient evidence of the scope of the problem. Successful investigations to date by U.S. attorneys, by the FBI, by HEW and various congressional committees have not given us any clear picture of the dimensions of organized crime activities in federal programs."

As we know, investigations and prosecutions in New York and Michigan have shown organized crime involvement to be a reality.

Griffin Bell's remarks were followed by the statement of the General Accounting Office before Pepper's committee. The headline of the statement read, "War on Organized Crime Faltering. Federal Strike Forces Not Getting the Job Done."

A more significant comment was made by Joseph H. Rodriguez, chairman of New Jersey's State Commission of Investigations. (Note: The Commission *investigates*. It doesn't prosecute.)

Rodriguez discussed the surveillance of health care rip-offs. He concluded, "Federal responsibility is simply not being lived up to." Michael R. Siavage, executive director of New Jersey's State Commission of Investigations, proceeded to cite chapter and verse. "Organized crime is, after all, defined as a continuing conspiracy for profit and power using fear and corruption and seeking, if possible, immunity from the law."

At the hearing before the Select Committee on Aging, the panel of law enforcement officers included, in addition to those from New Jersey, representatives from Florida, California, Michigan and Illinois. They were there to confirm that in their states, too, organized crime was riding high on health care money.

Representative William C. Wampler (R. Va.) cited a report released by Health, Education and Welfare Secretary Joseph Califano stating, "Estimated Medicaid losses for fiscal year 1977 were $2.5 billion out of an estimated expenditure of $9.8 billion." He also reported, "In the Medicare program, the estimated loss was $2.2 billion out of an estimated $21.9 billion. This is almost 12 per cent of total federal financing of these programs."

Wampler said, "If we combine Medicare and Medicaid with welfare, GSA [General Services Administration], CETA [Comprehensive Employment and Training Act] and other areas where mismanagement and crime are headline topics, the magnitude of tax loss is enormous. By its own estimates, HEW alone lost over $7 billion in fiscal year 1977.

"Let us put this staggering loss in a more understandable perspective," Wampler continued. "It amounts to all the federal income taxes paid by 5 million households earning $15,000 per year. It equals the total federal income tax paid by all residents in fifteen of our fifty states. It is $100 stolen every year from the pockets of 70 million U.S. taxpayers.

"The very fact that theft exists on such a massive scale

gives credence to the proposition that organized crime has invaded this field of federal domestic programs."

Representative Mario Biaggi (D. Bronx), chairman of the Sub-Committee on Human Services, added this statement:

"Health in many areas of this nation has been transformed from a service to a self-perpetuating profit industry. We are here today to learn how much of this profit goes to criminal elements through fraud in our largest federal health program—Medicare.

"What is most tragic is that we are, again, spotlighting the elderly as the crime victim—this time as a consumer. It is bad enough that we lose billions to fraud. But worse is the fact that these funds which should be used to fill the gaps in the Medicare program leave so many elderly totally unserved."

We here have statements which prove that organized crime and heartless nursing home owners are deeply into our pockets and tax money. We expect the federal government to do something about this. It is an ominous development.

This situation also puts it to us elders to check as we can into the sources of income among suppliers of health care. What we learn must be passed on to the FBI and to local government agencies which deal with organized crime. These agencies will work more effectively with our help.

Let's play a part in driving organized crime out of the nursing home and health care industries. We are the ones being hurt!

9

Elders in Adult Homes

In government circles, an adult home is called "adult care domiciliary facility." Translation—an adult home. It is defined in most states as a "facility for two or more adults who do not require [round the clock] medical or nursing care."

The definition goes on to state, "By reason of their age, infirmities or disabilities, they require lodging, board and housekeeping on a continuous basis. They also require immediate availability of personnel for recreation and social services; medication, supervision and assistance; along with nutritional service within the facility in which they reside."

Translation: If they need pills, the directors of the home must see to it that they take the right pills at the right time. If they get sick, a doctor or a nurse must be available. If they have special diets, they must not be permitted to eat food that isn't on the diets.

In most states, adult homes must display licenses.

The government definition continues, "A private proprietary home for adults shall mean, a facility operated for the purpose of providing suitable care therein for *compensation and profit.*"

These are the homes in which elders are placed when they're alone. It's where children place a parent or parents when a nursing home can't or won't accommodate them. It's where they go when discharged from a "health-related facility" or "skilled nursing facility" which may or may not be called nursing home. It's where elders are sent when they are discharged from mental hospitals.

In every state, there are many proprietary adult homes in which the proprietors are eager to obtain elders as residents. They *solicit* the business, paying a bonus for referrals even though that is against the law in many states. Adult home operation is a profitable business even when honestly conducted. It's a gold mine for those who know the sleazy tricks of the miserable trade.

We know about the scandal-ridden proprietary nursing home industry. Now add the proprietary adult home industry, where most of the scandals are not yet public. The reason for scandals is a lack of *specific* local or statewide regulatory provisions.

It is a good business, a profitable business. How can they miss? The less government supervision, the more profit. The less service, the more profit. The fewer the social programs, the more the profit. The less stringent the rules about fire and building safety, the more the profit. The fewer the numbers of inspections, the more the profit. The less personal or individual care, the more the profit. Like nursing homes, proprietary adult homes have become big business.

For example, in New York State the proprietaries were

mooching along in the ordinary way, providing housing for individual lonely old people who had no other place to go. Most were on welfare. Some were supported by relatives or partially so supported. Many were on Social Security or Supplemental Security Income (SSI).

Then came "deinstitutionalization" of mental patients in states throughout the country. In 1968, the New York State Department of Mental Hygiene transformed all chronic care mental institutions. They were to become hospitals—intensive care *hospitals*. They had, at the time, 80,321 patients.

The "deinstitutionalization" (a miserable word in every sense) called for a three-step policy.

1. Reduce the number of admissions to the mental institutions.
2. Shorten the length of stay at the mental institutions.
3. Discharge long-term mental patients.

No, the discharges weren't callous or arbitrary. Deinstitutionalization as a concept had won considerable support among hygienists in the mental health profession. Moreover, the policy saved the government a great chunk of money.

Between 1968 and 1977, the number of patients in New York State mental institutions, for example, decreased from 80,321 to 29,988. Most of these poor people ended up in proprietary adult homes. In fact, about 31 per cent of the statewide populations of the chronic care mental institutions ended up in proprietary adult homes. In New York City, for example, 44 per cent of dischargees were put in adult homes.

The adult homes, of course, were eager to take in the dischargees. This was their chance to make a bundle. They sailed into the situation because they were the *only* readily available places which could provide facilities for these unfortunates. Few other choices existed for state departments of mental hygiene.

Concurrently with the discharges, the mental hygiene departments intended to set up supportive community centers for dischargees. These were supposed to provide rehabilitative training. They were also supposed to assure a smooth transition into a normal life within the community.

In most states the departments of mental hygiene never got around to the rehabilitation part of the deinstitutionalization program. They didn't even go through the motions, nor did they formulate plans for community centers! The former mental patients were stashed in communities which didn't want them. They were placed in proprietary adult homes which did.

We call this a callous abandonment of patients. Is there any other name for it? Even if we agree that the patients should no longer stay in mental hospitals, does that mean that they are *prepared* to live alone in an adult home and in a hostile environment?

Ideally, adult home residents have a minimal need for special services. As a rule, they are ambulant, aware, lonely, normal in most respects. It is just that they are poor and old. But in the case of mental hospital dischargees, they need to readjust to normal situations and activities. For many years they've been "cared for." They're now on their own. They must relearn the techniques of caring for *themselves*.

Dischargees from mental institutions generally require special and thoughtful care. They have no place in the proprietary adult homes. Such homes are not in a position to help them readjust. Most proprietary adult homes are, in fact, totally unfit to serve former mental patients.

It is altogether a tragic situation. Each state mental hospital sets its own conditions for returning a patient to society. The use of adult homes for housing ex-patients aggravates a bad situation.

By law, adult homes may not provide nursing care or medical services. They have no trained personnel to monitor even such services as the policing of drug dosages. They cannot spot symptoms which may indicate that an ex-patient of a mental institution may become a danger to himself and others.

But the proprietary adult homes gleefully accepted these people as residents. Every new resident is more money in their pockets.

In New York State the licensing of proprietary adult homes is haphazard. Inspection of the homes and at the homes is cursory and limited. Proprietors of adult homes make their own rules. They have been given no explicit regulatory standards. That's true in most other states as well.

The proprietors decide on admissions. They pick their own staffs. They set their own activity program when they have programs. They ignore serious fire, safety and sanitary hazards.

A number of proprietors are concerned and responsible. They would welcome guidance. They would like to prove the importance of the role their facilities assume in the spectrum of adult care and support.

Discharged mental patients are lucky if they are placed in such good adult homes. There is a hope that they will be cared for with thoughtful consideration. They will be absorbed with other residents who are altogether normal. They will make good adjustments.

What are their chances of being placed in such good adult homes? Who can say? As we know, "A private proprietary home for adults means a facility housing two or more adults and operated for the purpose of providing suitable care therein for *compensation and profit*."

Forget that "two or more" bit. A proprietary adult home is usually a hotel or rooming house. It may be a converted apartment house. It may be a boardinghouse. Call it an adult home. It becomes an adult home!

Now we offer an important animadversion. A book of this kind requires a certain amount of active participation from serious readers. Don't shrug off the facts in this chapter. Don't say, "Oh well, that's how it goes in New York State." Some or all of the situations described and to be described in this chapter probably exist in adult homes in *your* own state.

What follows is a summary of problems and abuses met in proprietary adult homes statewide and in Nassau County, New York. This is what the Senior Citizens Project of the Nassau County Law Services Committee reports.

"Residents of proprietary adult homes may be thrown out into the streets. These people are simply put out the front door with all their belongings.

"They are discharged for non-payment. They are discharged when Social Security checks are delayed. There are no plans for admission to another facility. They are forced to leave the adult home without their own consent, without funds, without summary proceedings as prescribed by law.

"Intimidation is endemic in adult homes. Home owners in order to silence 'troublemakers' threaten to throw them out. These threats cause residents to remain in adult homes against their will. Their money is withheld by the owner of the home.

"The only income the residents get is Social Security or

SSI. The checks arrive in the adult home every month. The home proprietors open the residents' mail often without authorization.

"When residents inform the home that they would like to leave, they ask for the return of their Social Security checks. They are told, 'Sign over the checks to us or you will be thrown out. If you are discharged, your checks will be returned to the Social Security office.' Through past experience, the home owners are aware that a frail or mentally impaired resident will usually endorse the checks. Since the resident will be without funds for new housing, he or she will be 'persuaded' to endorse the check.

"Allegedly, only disruptive residents are thrown out. Although the alleged disruptive acts are subject to challenge by the resident, alternatives less harsh than discharge are seldom used.

"Residents are transferred without the resident's permission. Some home owners shift residents from one adult home to another where there are lower costs. The transfer may occur between homes run by the same owner or a different home owner. The switch is usually made for the benefit of the adult home owner rather than for the benefit of the elderly resident. The adult home owner pockets the difference between what it costs in one place and what it costs in the home to which the resident is switched.

"There is no 'model' admission contract or agreement which spells out the respective civil rights of the residents. Agreements are *imposed* on the residents. Therefore, residents have no bargaining power. In many cases, they cannot even negotiate a weekly spending allowance.

"Apparently many residents do not know how they arrived at the home. 'Someone picked me up and drove me here,' they say. In these cases it is likely that they had been 'solicited' by the home owner. The process of solicitation leads to serious and dangerous practices. Residents are being admitted to adult homes who may be medically ineligible. They have medical needs which an adult home cannot, by law, provide.

"Since home owners freely pick and choose their residents, a segregation of residents results. That produces a 'cesspool' effect. A caste system develops. Discharged mental patients and borderline discharged health-related facility seniors are denied admission in the 'better' homes. They are shunted into marginal homes. All the 'problem' residents live together. Thus their problems are aggravated.

"There are many instances of misuse and misappropriation by home owners of the residents' money. Those who have negotiated a spending allowance are often forced to agree to take the money 'in kind.' (A pack of cigarettes daily.) The resident doesn't receive an accounting of the money received. In many cases the daily allowance does not equal the monthly spending allowance agreed upon.

"Nor does the home owner provide an accounting of lump-sum Social Security checks and SSI payments sent to the residents. In New York State, Executive Law 758-a-3 (d) requires quarterly accounting. At this writing, few adult homes provide such an accounting.

"We find additionally that residents don't receive their Social Security or other official notices. Thus valuable appeal rights may be lost. If important mail is received and retained by the home owner, advocacy and other protective agencies should be informed.

"In matters of this kind, the home owner is acting on behalf of the resident without *authority*. Or he is failing to respond properly to the mailed notices. Or he is failing to contact the appropriate agency.

"Cheap tricks are the rule rather than the exception in many proprietary homes. During one Passover period, for example, Jewish residents were forced to pay a special 'Pesach Fee.' Residents complain of tipping. They read the 'No Tipping' signs. But they know that they must tip to get needed services.

"Other unfair adult home owner policies also create problems. Residents who move in after the first of a month or leave before the end of a month are charged for a full month's room and board. Residents who seek legal advice or need such advice find it difficult to get through to attorneys."

We have been describing the proprietary adult home situation in New York State. We believe similar conditions exist in proprietary, profit-making adult homes throughout the country. We are convinced that explicit regulatory standards should be promulgated, if possible nationally; certainly in individual states.

Specifically, and at a minimum, the following regulatory standards should govern relationships between adult home residents and the proprietors of adult homes:

1. A model contract should be designed. It should spell out the civil and personal rights of residents. When proprietors fail to observe all the terms of the contract, the residents, their advocates or their attorneys should be in a position to sue the home owner.

2. Ombudsman service should be available to prevent

proprietary adult home owners from withholding essential care and service.

3. Residents should be protected against being thrown out in the streets; or being neglected in their own rooms.

4. Building inspections should be made without prior notice. If the home owner does not correct fire and sanitary hazards immediately, he should be "delicensed" and put out of business.

5. Strict controls covering the dispensing of medications should be established.

6. Diversion of mail, expropriation of residents' funds should be ended.

7. Intimidation which discourages complaints to authorities and refusal to permit the intervention of outside advocacy personnel must end.

8. Transfers without solid proof that the transfer is necessary for the well-being of the resident should not be permitted.

9. A potential proprietary adult home resident discharged from a nursing home, a health-related facility or a mental institution should have a *choice* of at least three adult homes. These must be located in neighborhoods where the potential resident will be near relatives, friends or in familiar surroundings.

10. No proprietary adult home should be licensed which is not near medical services. These must include physician care, nursing, psychiatric, podiatric, dental, hospital and eye care. Physical, respiratory, occupational and speech therapy should also be readily available to residents.

Summing it up: The protection of the life, happiness and comfort of residents of adult homes is the responsibility of state and local governments. They must establish the strictest regulations. They must police these regulations.

Unless they do, we will have the same conditions in adult homes as now exist in nursing homes. Unless, therefore, adult home owners agree to these minimal conditions, they should *not* be licensed.

10

Second Interlude

"Nikka," I asked, "would you like to read the book as written so far?"

"How far is that?" she asked.

"Nine chapters."

"Hand it over," she said.

She started reading. I sat watching her, bug-eyed and tense. I was waiting for comment. Comment? Hell, I was waiting to hear her say, "Hurray for you!" I'd have settled for, "OK, it's fair."

Not a word. Nikka turned pages. Nikka picked up a pencil and made check marks as she read along.

That didn't bother me. Nikka has a sensitivity to writing which compares to the term "perfect pitch" in music. She spots incorrect word usage unerringly. She reacts immediately to an awkward formulation or an inept phrase. Whatever check marks she'd made were sure to improve the quality of the writing.

She flipped over the last page of the manuscript.

"I'll get to the check marks later," she said. "What bothers me about the whole thing is the name of the book."

"Now she tells me!" I exploded. "You were the one who sold me on the title. Or have you forgotten?"

"Yes, I know. It's still the right title—"

"But—"

She held up her hand like a traffic cop.

"Don't interrupt. You have nine chapters here. The title of the book contains the word 'rebellion.' Yet you don't provide a precise definition of what an *elderly rebel* must do to deserve the name."

"That's ridiculous," I blustered. "The definition of 'rebel' is established by suggestions throughout the manuscript."

"Not good enough," she countered. "That stuff in one of the chapters about minding the kids is no definition. You can't associate us seniors with 'rebellion' as the term is *normally* perceived. What are you suggesting? Mutiny? Disobedience? Revolt? Defiance? Insurrection?"

"OK, OK," I agreed reluctantly. "We're not fighting tyranny. We don't expect to challenge the system."

Nikka wouldn't let me off the hook.

"You should pin down as exactly as possible what you want seniors to do. Then you must explain what you expect the middle-aged pre-retirees to do. Explore the word 'rebel.'"

It turned out to be a difficult assignment. Readers can see what I'm up against. I went to the books for information and consolation.

"Look, Nikka, here's a bit about being old in Shakespeare's *Henry IV*."

She read the passage out loud. "'I could be well content to entertain the lag-end of my life with quiet hours.'"

"That may have been a good retirement idea for Shakespeare's time," I said. "But I don't think it applies now. It's just the opposite of what a rebel would say."

Nikka agreed. "You're right. So start with that. You know what an elderly rebel shouldn't say or do. Explain why and you're off to the races."

OK. I hereby challenge the Bard. There are certainly very few oldsters living in the last quarter of *this* century who are well content to entertain the lag-end of their lives with quiet hours. The times do not permit such an approach. Neither do our incomes.

Elderly poor are harassed by their poverty. Middle-income elderly are terrified by the thought that rising prices will make them poor. The elderly rich resent the loss of their prestige and status.

I read the paragraphs to Nikka. She smiled and said, "Work on it. I think I know where you're going." She then put on her coat and left me to my chore.

Let's develop the theme. We are not living in Shakespeare's day. We cannot value ourselves or judge our place in present-day society by the standards of the past. Each succeeding generation since the flood has established its own criteria for contentment, for honor, for acceptable behavior and for resistance.

A proper description of the situation of the populace in the early part of the nineteenth century was offered by Thoreau. In his book *Walden* Thoreau said, "The mass of men lead lives of quiet desperation."

Thoreau's incisive comment may not apply to the *mass* of men today. The young are not desperate. Nor are they quiet. But as a description of our lives as senior-agers today, Thoreau's summary hits it right on the nose.

In fact, the concept of "quiet desperation" brings us back directly to the "rebellion" situation. My bet is that Nikka will accept the following statement: Senior-agers are rebels when they struggle against conditions which *condemn* them to lives of quiet desperation.

Here we have a beginning for our essay on rebels. Social, economic and political authorities have defined the term for us. It is they who characterize non-conformity as rebellion. Non-conformers do not accept the term. Like beauty, rebelliousness is in the eye and mind of the beholder.

How could it be otherwise? The American colonists did not think of themselves as rebels when they protested King George's stamp tax. Did the early trade unionists consider themselves rebels when they fought for the eight-hour day? Did mildly left-thinking citizens act rebellious when they refused to name names to Joe McCarthy's committee?

History proves that the men and women who, *in their time*, were called "rebels" were in truth heroes. They were responsible for many, perhaps most, of the changes which improved the lives of peoples and nations.

That makes the title of this book valid. We older Americans believe that it is our right to live well. We demand that our years of contributing to society deserve to be rewarded in practical ways. We say, "Nothing is too good for the elderly." We chide our contemporaries when they fail to defend our interest.

On this issue we know that the authorities haven't chosen the word "rebel" for us. We, ourselves, have proudly named ourselves.

Rebels!

Nikka agreed.

11

Elders: Home Health Care I

There have been important changes in the rules and eligibilities for the delivery of our home health care. Until now, they've always been too strict, too limiting. Our job as activist elders is to make sure that officials in our own states, counties, cities and local political jurisdictions *implement* these changes.

We need to work on this basis. The *only* people who should stay in nursing homes are:

1. Those who are totally dysfunctional or disabled.
2. Those who have no suitable residence to which they can return when they escape from a nursing home.

All others (and their families) should consider the nursing home as a way station. The nursing homes serve until the specific illness or disability which put us into the nursing home clears up. Then, back we go to living independently in our own homes.

Home health, home help services are simply explained. They begin with visits by qualified or registered nurses working under doctors' orders. They include chore services such as preparing meals and cleaning the house. They arrange for transportation to hospitals or to physicians' offices.

There has been too much loose talk about home health help as an alternative to nursing homes. Not enough thought has been given to home help as an *option* to nursing homes. That is because home health care services have never been precisely *defined*. Many elders and their families now believe that "institutionalization" should be the *alternative*. Home health services should be an *option*.

The Medicare amendments of 1978 made the following important changes in the home health/home help rules. A review of these rules indicate that they had been altogether too strict.

> First, neither Medicare nor Medicaid would pay for home health help/care unless the patient had been hospitalized for a minimum of three days.

> Secondly, the plan of home care had to be prescribed by a physician. The nursing care ordered had to be "skilled." The patient had to be home-bound.

> Third, under hospital insurance, home visits were limited to one hundred per calendar year.

As a result of these tight rules, many of us did not *dare* to leave nursing homes. We may have felt that we could "make it" back in our own homes. But in addition to skilled nursing care, administered under doctor's orders, we needed other *kinds* of help. There were housekeeping chores to be done. There were meals to be prepared. There was the ever-present and serious problem of loneliness for widows and widowers among us.

The doctor determined how the one hundred permissible

skilled care visits should be used. But who decided how much assistance in addition to medical help was necessary? We must face the issue squarely. With home help and chore service, we could live independently. Without such help we would have been forced back to the nursing home. There was nothing in between.

The 1978 amendments changed all that. Among the important improvements in the home health benefits were the following:

1. Unlimited visits would be available under both Parts A and B of Medicare.

2. The three-day prior hospitalization requirement under Part A would be eliminated.

3. Home health benefits under Part B would no longer be subject to $60 deductible.

4. Presumed coverage provisions and provisions that limit reimbursement to the provider of services were altered. Where these charges were unreasonable, they would be lowered.

In addition, the Department of Health, Education and Welfare would get new authority. HEW would be on orders to establish new standards and reimbursement guidelines for more effective local and national administration of home health benefits. HEW would also be assigned the task of designating regional intermediaries for home health agencies.

(Note: The bill in the House of Representatives, H.R. 13097, had the above provisions. Some, but not all, of these provisions were approved in Senate bill S. 5285. At the conference of both houses agreement was not achieved prior to the adjournment of the 95th Congress.)

Now an update:

Washington, D.C., May 3, 1979. House Aging Committee Chairman Claude Pepper (D. Fla.) has charged HEW with grossly neglecting the needs of the 7 million Americans who urgently require home health services to avoid consignment to nursing homes or costly, unnecessary hospital stays.

Pepper's comments came in response to a departmental report on in-home services under Medicare, Medicaid and social services mandated by Congress in 1977.

"We gave the Secretary a full year to produce a report on home health care," said Pepper, "and that report was to include recommendations for legislative and administrative changes in this crucial area. Congress waited, in full faith, for the report to be issued, and now—six months after the legal deadline—they have sent a document that is extraordinary for its negativism, timidity and calculating ambiguity," he continued.

Sec. 18 of Public Law 95-142 (the Medicare-Medicaid Anti-Fraud and Abuse Amendments) required the Secretary of HEW to give Congress a report "analyzing, evaluating, and making recommendations with respect to all aspects . . . of the delivery of home health and other in-home services. . . ." Beyond indications that a few administrative changes affecting program operations would be made, the report *stopped short of recommending legislative action,* citing budgetary restraints.

"Studies by the General Accounting Office and others have cited the cost-effectiveness of home health compared with nursing home care," observed Pepper. "We should move forward now with those changes in the law which would cost little or even save money. And there are many revisions which should be made in the future, when the economic climate allows. HEW claims to support expanded home health but has failed even to establish long-term goals

—goals to which the President committed himself in the 1976 campaign.

"Time and again the HEW report mentions the need, for example, of expanding access to in-home care in underserved areas. Yet the administration proposes, in the fiscal year 1980 budget, to wipe out the major government program which could solve this problem—Public Health Service grants to establish or expand home health agencies, particularly in areas with high concentrations of elderly or medically needy. And there are some 650 counties—where almost 10 million people live—which do not have a Medicarecertified home health agency.

"There is strong support in the Congress for allowing many more Medicare recipients to receive home health care. Last year, both the House and Senate passed my proposals to remove the prior hospitalization requirement under the hospital insurance program (Part A) and eliminate the limit on visits. Unfortunately, these provisions were held hostage to the hospital cost-containment controversy. But the mood of Congress is clear. I am confident the Congress will pass home health changes under Medicare. I am hopeful HEW will ultimately support the needed amendments." (The Pepper reference was to H.R. 13097, Medicare amendments, which passed the House 398–2, and H.R. 5285, which passed the Senate, but with hospital cost-containment provisions.)

Pepper has again introduced Medicare home health expansion legislation, H.R. 2567, which would remove the requirement of prior hospitalization under Part A, remove the "homebound" requirement, delete the visit limits, eliminate the requirement that care be "skilled," add homemaker and chore services, remove the Part B (supplementary medical insurance) deductible for home health and make other changes.

"The Department's report is inconsistent with the mandate of Congress," said Pepper. "We keenly regret that HEW has not taken a stronger leadership position. We asked them for guidance in making home health care more available to our people, and, instead, they gave us a discourse on the problems which exist."

Here are the reasons why we activist elders should launch drives to get the U. S. Senate to approve *all* these provisions in the 96th Congress.

During the autumn of 1976, the Department of Health, Education and Welfare held five regional hearings on the subject of home health care. Reports to these hearings covered broad areas of home-delivered services to elders.

Those who spoke at the hearings included certified home health agencies and Homemaker Home Health Aide services. Support services such as "meals on wheels" and other related interests also testified. The issues ranged from cost containment to the quality of care.

The hearing summary states:

"The primary concern expressed by the witnesses was for an expanded, coordinated range of high-quality home services as a part of an essential continuum of health care, social and support services. The greatest consensus about expanded benefits was for broader coverage of Homemaker Home Health Aide services by all third-party payment programs.

"A second area of consensus was the need to include transportation services, home-delivered meals, nutrition services, and mechanisms for coordinating the delivery of round-the-clock services at the local level . . . The need to eliminate artificial distinctions between health and social services was also strongly urged by many witnesses." (From an article by Florence M. Moore in the magazine *Public Welfare* of the American Public Welfare Association.)

Homemaker Home Health Aide, Inc. (HHHA) plays an important part in the continuum of health care to elders. But if you want a picture of utter government and managerial confusion, the HHHA is it. The control is supposed to be under state direction. The townships, villages, cities and other jurisdictions participate in the action.

Until the new benefits take effect, no one has clarified the costs. No one has set standards for performance.

The National Council for Homemaker Home Health Aide, Inc. reports, "Where such standards have been set they are generally ignored."

The funding and financial resources can range anywhere from Medicare and Medicaid to grants from a long list of foundations. Regulatory and accounting procedures were loose, indefinite. Home help services were indifferently policed. In short, it was an unholy mess. As a result, we elders suffered.

As this situation continued it was safe to offer a dismal prophecy. Unless protective procedures in home health care are improved, we're building up to a massive scandal in the HHHA. It will be equal to and possibly worse than the already exposed and still continuing scandals in nursing homes. We think that it is still safe to make such a prophecy. Let's look into the possibilities.

In home health/home help services, the "for profit services" will not be the only culprits. The "not for profit" services may also be involved in various abuses and frauds. We cite just one report.

The policing of Homemaker Home Health Aide, Inc. is difficult. Florida offers an example of what may become a scandal. In that state there has been a proliferation of *private* not-for-profit HHHA agencies.

They are privately owned. They are officially incorporated as "not for profit." They are not to be confused with bona fide not-for-profit agencies such as visiting nurse and family service agencies.

There is no basis on which the state of Florida can refuse certification either of proprietary or of non-profit agencies. Many of these private HHHAs are "Medicare only" agencies. Medicare pays 100 per cent of the patient's costs.

According to a Blue Cross memorandum of June 1976, complaints (about the private "Medicare only" agencies) include the following: There is excessive staffing. There are exorbitant salary payments. Add high automobile expenses and kickbacks for referrals and the dismal picture is *still* not complete.

The Florida Blue Cross complains as follows: In determining allowable costs for HHHAs there are no restrictions in the law or in the regulations. There are no guidelines or reimbursement manuals to assist Blue Cross to determine what salaries or fringe benefits for management should be considered "reasonable."

Other states may have similar complaints. But we'll stick to Florida because so many elders live there. Proposals by Blue Cross of Florida covered the following:

1. Guidelines should be developed for salaries, number and type of positions, fringe benefits for executives. Maximum cost or charge per visit should also be set up.

2. Qualifications for a full-time administrator should be established.

3. Legislation should be developed for certificate of *need* for new HHHAs.

4. A regulation should be ordered for providers to be certified under medical programs only if they agree to accept patients *without regard to the method of payment.*

5. The state should permit intermediaries to have budget approvals over home health agencies.

Standards of performance have not been defined for the so-called non-profit home health agencies either. Can we expect the growing number of proprietary (for profit) agencies to toe any lines at all?

Florida's Blue Cross complaints and suggestions for improvement are all problems of *fiscal* manipulations. Over the nation, we elders and our families are less concerned with money than we are with the *kind* of help we receive.

In 1976, the Department of Health, Education and Welfare held regional hearings. Five hundred or more people testified at these hearings. Nearly all speakers raised the question of "quality in-home care."

Back in 1975 when HEW published the Medicaid regulations on home care, they permitted the proprietary agencies to participate in the program. But at that time, the government set no standard of performance or types of personnel to be involved. There was no way to police either the proprietaries or the not-for-profit operators. Guidelines were lacking in all the matters which concern in-home services for us elders.

Basic differences exist between the *quality* of home care and the investment in home care. The National Council for Homemaker Home Health Aide, Inc. proposed a set of standards to protect us elders and other home care consumers.

First the Council set up a National Advocacy Advisory Committee. National voluntary organizations and foundations were represented on the committee. These national groups involved their local affiliates in the areas chosen for demonstration. Their job was to cooperate with the project activities on state and local levels. Funding was through the Administration on Aging (AoA) with some financial assistance from Exxon Corporation.

To this broad base were added directors and staff members of local and state offices of the aging and directors of social and health services. This group established the elements of the teamwork by the professionals who would oversee and, in some cases, manage local home health/home help services.

Note that the title of the Council's advisory committee uses the word "advocacy." The position of an advocate in any situation is that of a checker-upper who usually is an interested volunteer who seeks to protect the interests of *consumers*. A voluntary advocate in each community where a Council project is established selects two or more assistant volunteers. All are trained to understand the details of services. They rally interest in home health aid and push to develop more effective in-home services. They act as ombudspersons for the consumers and for their families.

The National Council's Advocacy project is not alone in this effort to provide a continuum of home help and health services to the aged. The National Council on the Aging (NCOA) has a steering committee of national voluntary organizations. They work for "older persons living in their own homes." Committee chairperson is Dr. Ellen Winston, former welfare commissioner of HEW. She was also past president of the National Council for Homemaker Home Health Aide, Inc.

The NCOA has been on this job since the 1971 White House Conference on the Aging. In 1974, it received a three-year grant and set up a project known as Operation Independence. How successful has it been?

We return to Dr. Winston's comment at the same hearings covered by Florence M. Moore in the magazine *Public Welfare* of the American Public Welfare Association.

Here is what Dr. Winston reports in the NCOA magazine *Perspective on Aging* (May/June 1978):

"The primary concern expressed by the witnesses was for an expanded continuum of health, social and support services. The greatest consensus about expanded benefits was for broader coverage of homemaker/home health aide services by all third-party payment programs.

"A second area of consensus was the need to include transportation services, home-delivered meals and nutrition services, and some mechanism for coordinating the delivery of round-the-clock services at the local level.

"Pleas for elimination of artificial barriers to obtaining needed home services were a recurrent theme throughout the hearings. . . . The need to eliminate artificial distinctions between health and social services was also strongly urged by many witnesses.

"The need for coordination of the delivery of services at the local level was one of the most insistent themes presented by the witnesses."

Here are two prestigious organizations, the National Council for HHHA, and the National Council on the Aging (NCOA). Along with other independent voluntary groups, they work to expand home health and home help services for the aged. How does it happen, therefore, that as reported in 1976, there were approximately five thousand home health/home help aides in the entire country? Is it conceivable that so small a number could administer to the needs of our approximately 200 million elders?

The Netherlands, for example, with a population of only 13.5 million older people, has about the same number of home health aides as we have.

In a typical month in the province of Manitoba, Canada, 1,500 homemakers are employed to deliver services to 3,636 citizens.

We compare figures like these with what happens in the United States. Shouldn't we be ashamed of ourselves?

The National Council for Homemaker Home Health Aide, Inc. has issued a pamphlet entitled, *14 Standards Basic to Safe and Efficient (Homemaker/Home Health) Services*. With permission of the Council, we submit the fourteen points without emendation or comments.

1. The agency shall have legal authorization to operate.

2. There shall be an appropriate, duly constituted authority in which ultimate responsibility and accountability are lodged.

3. There shall be no discriminatory practices based on race, color or national origin. The agency must have or be working toward an integrated board, advisory committee, Homemaker Home Health Aide services staff, and clientele.

4. There shall be designated responsibility for the planning and provision of financial support to main-

tain current level of service on a continuing basis.

5. The service shall have written personnel policies; a wage scale shall be established for each job category.

6. There shall be a written job description for each job category for all staff and volunteer positions which are part of the service.

8. There shall be an appropriate process utilized in the selection of homemaker home health aides.

10. There shall be a written statement of eligibility criteria for the service.

11. The service, as an integral part of the community's health and welfare delivery system, shall work toward assuming an active role in an ongoing assessment of community needs and in planning to meet these needs including making appropriate adaptations in the service.

12. There shall be an ongoing agency program of interpreting the services to the public, both lay and professional.

13. The governing authority shall evaluate through regular systematic review all aspects of its organization and activities in relation to the service's purposes and to community needs.

14. Reports shall be made to the community, and to the National Council for Homemaker Home Health Aide, Inc., as requested.

There's more to this home health/home help proposition. Read the next chapter carefully.

12

Elders: Home Health Care II

You may ask, "What happened to standards 7 and 9? Why did we skip these two standards for home health/home help aides in the previous chapter? Are they not considered basic to safe and efficient home health services? All the standards of performance are important. This author believes, however, that standards 7 and 9 deserve special emphasis. Here they are:

7. Every individual and/or family served shall be provided with the following two essential components of the service:

A. Service of a homemaker home health aide and supervisor.

B. Service of a professional person responsible for assessment and implementation of a plan of care.

This standard represents the "heart" of Homemaker Home Health Aide service. It argues that Homemaker

Home Health Aide service is a *team* service which includes both the professional and all Homemaker Home Health Aide personnel in an agency.

Functions of a professional supervisor should include:

1. In-person (home or office) assessment and periodic reassessment of the need for Homemaker Home Health Aide service.

2. Development of a *plan of care* which includes all aspects of services that are required. All clients should have available input from qualified social workers, qualified health professionals and other professionals as needed.

3. Providing the homemaker home health aide with the plan for service delivery and periodic home visits by the *supervisor* to see that the plan is being carried out and is appropriate.

4. Individual conferences with the homemaker home health aide to discuss service and, in the interim times, telephone discussions to maintain contact with the aide.

5. Maintenance of complete and appropriate records about the service being delivered to the client and complete records about the homemaker home health aide's performance. These must include a formal evaluation on a periodic basis.

6. Convening of an interdisciplinary conference which includes the homemaker home health aide. The purpose here is to discuss the individual's and the family's needs.

7. Plans for the appropriate termination of service.

The homemaker home health aide has the responsibility for carrying out the tasks outlined in the plan of care. He or she must be aware of changes as they may occur in the needs of the individual or family and report these changes to the professional team member.

The professional team member should have qualifications appropriate to the situation. Nursing supervision must be available in situations where personal care is part of a medical plan. Nursing care or consultation must be available where personal care is provided as supportive assistance. Social work supervision or consultation must be available where there are psychological or social problems. The home management skills of the home economist are often needed and should be available where appropriate.

Professional staff members who function in Homemaker Home Health Aide service shall have as a minimum the following qualifications as appropriate:

". . . a current license to practice as a registered professional nurse; a bachelor's degree in social work, home economics (or a closely related helping profession), plus one year of related experience."

We learn from number 7 in the basic standards of services that home health service calls for a *team* effort. It explains the minimum qualifications required for those who participate as leaders of the team. Now let's get to basic standard number 9:

9. There shall be: a) initial generic training for homemaker home health aides such as outlined in the National Council for Homemaker Services' Training Manual; b) an ongoing in-service training program for homemaker home health aides.

The initial and ongoing training of homemaker home health aides is an essential component of the standards.

Initial generic training shall be a minimum of forty hours and should be provided prior to, or at least within the first six months of, employment. The forty hours are to include formal classroom instruction and supervised laboratory instruction in the following areas:

1. The agency, the community and the homemaker home health aide
2. The family and the homemaker home health aide
3. Care and maintenance of the home and personal belongings
4. Home accident prevention
5. Family spending and budgeting
6. Food, nutrition and meals
7. The child in the family
8. The ill, the disabled and the aging adult
9. Mental health and mental illness
10. Personal care and rehabilitative services

Qualified individuals from a variety of disciplines shall be utilized as instructors in their areas of expertise. Training by health professionals alone, by social workers or by home economists alone will not suffice. On-the-job training is in addition to the forty hours of classroom and laboratory training.

In-home service training programs should be offered on a regularly scheduled ongoing basis, at least quarterly. All homemaker home health aides should have the opportunity to attend these meetings. The programs should follow up content areas introduced in the initial generic training and include relevant trends in service. Programs on the agency's policies and procedures are necessary but should not constitute the majority of programs. Opportunity to attend outside seminars and workshops should be made available.

As the number of Homemaker Home Health Aide staff increases, the agency should develop vertical and/or horizontal job opportunities which recognize competence and skill.

Here in these two chapters we have the whole set of standards. We grant that the Council presents it as an *"Interpretation* of Standards for Homemaker Home Health Aide services." But it's worth careful study. It is the very *first* specific analysis of what's needed. It covers the quality and training of *personnel.* It relates to the delivery of Homemaker Home Health Aide services. It gives us a reasonable blueprint of what the elderly are entitled to in the Homemaker Home Health Aide field.

Now we pose the challenge: Name one state, name one city, name one county in which any or most of these standards exist. Name one political jurisdiction in the entire United States where we elders can actually live *independently* in our own homes before or after institutionalization in a nursing home.

Is it not true that throughout the nation, Homemaker Home Health Aide services in most areas often operate on a catch-as-catch-can basis? Many such programs are merely gestures.

To explain this we need to understand the psychology involved. This country, at least the Department of Health, Education and Welfare, is all gung ho about nursing homes.

That is understandable. When elders are entirely dysfunctional, a nursing home should be the rule. But all possible protective, medical and rehabilitation services should be available.

But not *all* elders are *totally* disabled. Therefore, there must be some provision, some escape for those elders who need *temporary* nursing and home health service. The General Accounting Office (GAO) understands this. They have documented the advantages of expanding *home health* benefits for elders in preference to nursing homes.

The GAO report entitled "Home Health—The Need for a National Policy Better to Provide for the Elderly" concludes, "Until older people become greatly or extremely impaired, *the cost of nursing homes exceeds* the cost of home care."

We have seen that current Medicare home health requirements prevent many elderly and partially disabled senior citizens from receiving home care services. Older people who live alone have, of course, a higher probability of institutionalization. Those living with spouses or children do not. Thirty-one per cent of people who are greatly (even temporarily impaired) live alone. Seventy-six per cent of them are required to enter institutions.

A Health, Education and Welfare study indicates that between 14 and 25 per cent of institutionalized elders may not *need* institutional care! Yet in 1976 only about 1 per cent of more than $3 billion in Medicaid funds used for persons over sixty-five was spent on home care. This compares with 70 per cent for care in intermediate and skilled nursing homes.

Additionally, only about 10 per cent of Medicare Part A funds was spent for home health care. About 1 per cent of Part B funds paid home health bills.

We cannot leave the "money" question yet. We must consider the dollar value of services provided by family and friends. On all counts, that kind of financial and service help is significantly higher than public agency costs.

We know now that the main stumbling blocks to the extension of home health care could be removed. "Prior hospitalization" should no longer be required as a basis for getting home health care. Ditto the maximum number of home visits per year.

The need remains to force the states to insist that home health services, both the for-profit and the not-for-profit, be licensed in order to be eligible for Medicare. A second need would be to include additional services in home health care. These would be periodic chore assistance, hospital outreach such as day care, and home-delivered meals.

What would such changes amount to in money? We go back to the GAO report for the fiscal year 1978. The cost of eliminating *limits* on home visits would be $12.5 million, a mere 2 per cent increase in home health benefit costs. Eliminating the *prior hospitalization* requirement would also cost $12.5 million. Adding homemaker and other chore service would cost another $75 million.

Congressman Pepper of the Select Committee on Aging declares, "This would be a small price to pay. It would be cost-effective. It would be a significant start toward reducing the $120 *billion* national health cost now being paid to support the *institutional bias* of the federal government."

In analyzing the GAO report, *Aging* magazine (published by the Department of Health, Education and Welfare—Nos. 281–282 of March-April 1978) expresses its concern as follows:

"The report also points to the proliferation and fragmentation of home health services.

"There is general agreement among state and local

officials that 'there are indeed a vast number of services available.' There are many different programs. Effective coordination and delivery of all home health care is difficult. But such coordination would not be impossible."

Officials have also noted that many *physicians* were unaware of the types of services provided by home health agencies. Nor do all states have the same requirements for the number of home visits allowed under Medicaid.

Let's go into that. Under current legislation various federal home health programs cannot be coordinated, according to HEW. An overall federal policy for home health care would have to be developed and legislative changes enacted before the programs could be consolidated.

The General Accounting Office report recommended that HEW:

- Have intermediaries and carriers publicize home health care and provide information concerning the availability of these services to physicians, hospitals and institutional providers.
- Identify state Medicaid programs which do not provide equal treatment to eligible individuals and take steps to correct such inequities.
- Develop a comprehensive national home health policy for consideration by the Congress.

For three years now Congressman Pepper and his assistants have pleaded with HEW. They have asked that HEW set standards for home health care. They have literally *begged* for such a national program.

Senator Church of the Special Committee on Aging of the United States Senate has also spoken critically about the loose operation, delivery and supervision of Homemaker Home Health Aide services.

The indifference and dilatory approach to Homemaker Home Health Aide services by the HEW is difficult to understand. The fact that the Administration on Aging has *permitted* such delaying tactics is, to many of us, totally unbelievable!

What is holding up the works here? Whose ox will be gored if HEW sets firm, effective and expanded standards for Homemaker Home Health Aide care for us elders? In what other field of federal money distribution do such loose, even careless conditions apply? HEW regulations are minimal. Guidelines are practically non-existent.

To begin with, we have the fifty states, which resent specific federal rules, regulations and guidelines. The states want to act on their own. That permits political maneuvers. These benefit the party in power. But they do not, as a rule, serve the interests of the elders who need Homemaker Home Health Aide assistance.

Follow this resentment against rules and regulations down the line to city and county governments. You get a picture of chaotic performance across the nation in the Homemaker Home Health Aide field.

The time has come for the *average American* to support the congressional forces urgently pushing for federal standards in home care. Volunteerism on a local basis is not enough. With the best will in the world, volunteers will not achieve major or significant successes in this field. We elders are virtually *unprotected* when the work of volunteers in various jurisdictions depends on *local* decisions politically administered.

HEW allots and distributes the funds for home health

care to the states. HEW should, therefore, set up standards for the states. The standards of quality performance should be spelled out. The regulations should be clear, unequivocal and precise. Not one dollar should go to any state which does not conform to regulations. Obviously, neither the House nor the Senate can swing this on its own. They need the backing of large numbers of Americans of all ages who understand what needs to be done.

We elders call upon our middlescent sons and daughters to organize campaigns for practical Homemaker Home Health Aide programs. Together we can move HEW to act in the interest of all elders who wish to live independently in their own homes.

Pressure will be necessary. Organization will be necessary. Nationally, the American Association of Retired Persons should act on this issue. So should the National Council of Senior Citizens. Defensive and activist groups of elders in cities, counties and villages should have Homemaker Home Health Aide services on their agendas. Our congressmen and senators should be receiving a constant flow of letters demanding action on this issue. Copies of all communications should be sent to HEW.

Three years is too long to wait for a set of defined standards, rules and regulations covering in detail Homemaker Home Health Aide services for elders.

Our right to independence in our own homes is not in question. The program must be conducted on a national basis. It will be a struggle. We have the backing of the National Council for Homemaker Home Health Aide, Inc. We can count on the support of the National Council on the Aging. But we elders and our sons and daughters should take local leadership in this important drive to assure workable Homemaker Home Health Aide programs. It requires organization. It will call for local activism.

This is a battle we can *win*.

13

Elders and Housing

A little nostalgia.

Most of us who are now in our sixties and seventies didn't have much to roar about during the Roaring Twenties. Men and women were concerned with getting jobs. We were trying to "make good" and hold on to the jobs we had. Men were building careers. Except for teachers and other professionals, women who are now our age just worked at any kind of job they could get.

We were also getting married. In those days we men didn't marry until we could support a wife. The custom was for women to leave their jobs right after the wedding. Their sister employees chipped in for a gift and a farewell party.

Some wives continued to work after marriage. They were the ones who wanted to save money for the baby-to-come. They became pregnant. Then they quit their jobs.

The first city apartment shared with our new wives had three rooms; kitchen, bedroom, living room. The crib of the first baby was kept in the bedroom next to our bed.

A year or two later came the second baby. We moved to larger quarters. Now the first baby had a room of its own. The second baby took over in our room for a while. Then it shared the first child's room.

When our families increased, the question of space again became important. There are only two sexes. When they were little, it was possible to crowd three children in one room, especially if they were all the same sex. But they grew up. If they were of opposite sexes the need for extra space again demanded attention. We moved again. This time to a four- or five-room apartment. Prices then ran from $45 to $75 per month depending on the neighborhood, the size of the rooms and the closet space.

Some of us have lived in apartments all our lives. We were said to have come "up" in the world when we moved from walk-ups to buildings with elevators and fancy foyers. They were located in "better" neighborhoods. This was the beginning of upward mobility for those of us who were considered "successful."

While we were working, life was good. We paid our rent on time. We watched our children grow. Our income covered most necessary expenses. In those days, a doctor's visit cost $2.00 or $3.00 (paid on the spot). Food, clothing and other necessities were cheap. For many of us the good old days *were* good old days. Prosperity is easy to take.

How the apartment house dwellers and homeowners among us came through the depression is another story. Literally, we eked out the rent money. There were "rent parties." There were kindly landlords. Say that we struggled through.

However, homeowners among us were into the banks for mortgage money. The banks and the insurance companies foreclosed. Seeing a family's possessions on the street brought a "There but for the grace of God go I." Sympathetic people were unable to help. The expropriated homeowners crowded in with parents or relations or friends. Life went on. We shared space.

When the rough times eased up a peculiar thing happened. Apartment dwellers swore that they'd never again pay rent. They were going to build equity in homes of their own. Those who had owned homes and lost them were, for a time, more careful. They had been burned by home ownership. It took them a long time to get up the courage to try again to be homeowners.

The situation settled in the middle and late thirties. The building boom was mostly a matter of private home development on the edge of cities. There was also building action in the nearby suburbs. The former apartment dwellers bought homes.

Meanwhile both groups were growing older. They had reached their early middle years. They were settled. They had jobs. Some had started saving money. The trade unions had won gains for their members. The AFL-CIO had become a factor in production. Industrial unionism had won out against craft unionism. Everybody felt safe.

In those years you could get a mortgage at 5 per cent. Prices for homes began at $8,500 for small semi-detached properties in the cities' outskirts. The prices went from $12,500 to $20,000 for larger seven-room houses in the burgeoning nearby suburbs. Additionally, factories were making their appearance in areas marked for industry away from the cities.

By the time World War II began, the movement toward home ownership had developed considerable momentum. It was possible for many of us middle-income folk in our early or late thirties to become homeowners. We would bring up our children in an environment suited to our income. We would send them on to college.

We reached our forties, our fifties, our sixties. Those who had stayed as renters in their apartments saw their neighborhoods deteriorate. If they had enough money for a down payment on a house, they bought a home in the suburbs. If not, they rented in a more suitable apartment in a better neighborhood.

The rent control laws, however, limited their choices both of neighborhoods and apartments. Rent was controlled for those already occupying apartments. When a family moved, the new rent could become prohibitive. Often it did. Only the rich could move from neighborhoods where the properties were likely to become run-down all the way to slums.

A majority of city elders now live either in run-down apartments or shabby private houses which need painting or repairs. We deserve better. In fact, we deserve the best. We are the people who built up the communities in which we now live.

Our taxes paid for the schools in the cities and suburbs. Our cultural interests supported and built the concert halls, the art galleries, the museums, the social centers. Our religious activities maintained the churches and the synagogues. Through organization and strike action we built our unions.

We fought in two wars. We sent our sons and daughters to the front lines in Korea and Vietnam. Our wives took our places in factories and offices. *This country owes us!*

Our dedicated services to our nation, our cities and our communities have brought meager reward indeed.

Let's get down to cases. The lack of money is the root of all the housing evils from which we suffer. Retirement cuts our income in half. This, at a time when prices for everything are up. In the cities, the elderly have a choice of buying food or paying rent. In the suburbs it's a question of buying food or paying property tax. The news releases which report that many of us are eating dog food are true.

Our situation as homeowners in the suburbs is especially dicey. Here we are, two old people. We rattle around in six, seven or eight rooms. Will the housing authorities let us rent out rooms? Will they permit us to change the house from a one-family to a two-family house?

They won't. The zoning laws have established our homes forever as one-family dwellings.

It was proposed, for example, that elderly residents be permitted to redesign their houses for two apartments. The agreement would be written so that only another *elderly* couple could rent the upstairs apartment in the redesigned building.

The author of this book offered that proposal in his own county. His proposal included an agreement. "When the elder *owners* died, the house would be re-established as a single-family unit. Or it would be occupied forever by two *elderly* couples."

The outcry throughout Nassau and Suffolk counties (New York) was unbelievable! "Single-family zoning," the housing and zoning authorities declared, "is sacred. It is the sine qua non of suburban living."

"From a social and humane standpoint," I pointed out, "the special value of the proposal has much to offer the elderly." Inevitably, one of the residents would die. The presence of elderly neighbors in the same building would be a comfort to the bereaved. After all, both elderly couples shared the same understanding of the inevitability of death.

That thought didn't move the housing authorities either. I tried another appeal. At the time I was pushing this project (1973) the elementary and high school population was growing. Schools were getting crowded. New schools had been and were being built all over both counties with our tax money.

My assurance that elders in two-family houses would not have children in schools didn't sway the housing authorities either. They repeated, "The zoning laws state one family to a house. No exceptions permitted."

Another appeal concerned money. In a two-family house, one pays rent. The other pays property taxes. The income from the rental of an apartment pays a good part toward the property tax for the renter. It also covers repairs. The money realized from the sale of their home by the elderly rentee pays the rent.

At today's resale prices, a good solid house, even in shabby condition, can be sold. Often it can be sold at a price twice what the house had cost twenty-five years ago. The elders who choose to sell can live in moderate comfort before they need to dip either into earlier savings or into their Social Security.

The truth of the matter is that a number of elders have already begun breaking the single-family zoning laws. Housing authorities in many suburban counties over the country are permitting this to happen in many communities. They are realists. But there is always the danger of a crackdown.

Activist organizations of elders should, therefore, start campaigning for "legitimization" of the two-families-of-elders-per-house "idea." The key word here is "elders."

Elders would be the *only* citizens who would participate in this change of the zoning law. Limitations of various kinds could be set up. One such limitation might be the number of seniors who could occupy the house. Another might be to specify age sixty or sixty-five for occupancy of both apartments. A third condition might be that the owners spend a specific sum of money to put the house in better shape.

We speak here of private housing. For many years now the federal government through HUD (the Department of Housing and Urban Development) has been offering money to local governments to be used for apartment buildings or other types of residences for the elderly. The problem there is that the money offered is tied in with the building of "low-income" housing as well.

Nationally, township supervisors and county officials (especially in the suburbs) are refusing the money. They say that they'll take the money for housing for the elderly. But they don't want the low-income people in their communities. Their arguments? "We don't want slums." Read that as follows: "We don't want blacks. We don't want poor people. We don't really want the elderly, either. We'll use the poor as an excuse *not* to build housing for elders."

This brings us to federal housing assistance plans, notably HUD's Section 8. Single elders whose monthly income ranges between $250 to $500 per month pay only 25 per cent of their rental costs. Elderly couples whose income is between $550 and $800 per month also pay 25 per cent of their rental costs. The government pays the rest.

But here's the catch. The landlord must *agree* to accept the listed government rent figures from elders. These run between $227 per month to $334 per month. The required rentals are based on non-elevator buildings. There are very few livable apartment buildings which have no elevators.

The elderly who live in privately owned apartments with elevators have two strikes against them. Most landlords grant only one-year leases to older residents. This is a blatant form of discrimination. It makes them subject to constant fear. Rents will go up. Don't they always?

There are, for example, 200,000 people in Nassau County over age sixty. There are only three thousand apartment units designated as "senior citizen" housing. In the town of Hempstead, at this writing, there are six thousand applications by elders for admission to the twenty-two senior housing developments. Other suburban communities in the Long Island counties report similar numbers of applications for government-supported or government-built senior housing!

It is the same in suburbs throughout the nation. The Nassau County Department of Senior Citizen Affairs supplies a check list of criteria for senior citizen housing. It turns out to be an exercise in futility.

The check list has fifteen points. It begins with "Senior housing developments should be located in residential or commercial areas, but not in hard-to-reach, hard-to-service isolated areas." From there the fifteen points cover everything needed to assure comfort for elders. These include convenience to hospitals, clinics and multi-purpose centers, shopping areas, religious institutions, recreation areas, etc. The points even mention outdoor sitting areas, recreation areas and places for outdoor cooking.

Actually, we elders would be wonderfully accommodated if such housing were to be built and if rentals related to a proper proportion of income.

But as we pointed out earlier, few construction companies

are building such housing. The town officials insist on getting government money for such developments without consideration of the need for the tie-in for low-income housing.

Here we are, then. We, the elders. Homeowners among us are hung up by spiraling property taxes. We pay high utility rates. We have no money to paint or to make repairs in the old homes we have occupied throughout our adult lives.

As a result of the recalcitrance of town officials, our housing situation is often critical. Hundreds of thousands of us are forced to live in a substandard environment. Everything is too expensive. Our homes are impossible to maintain. They are also overadequate for our needs.

We call, therefore, for larger government subsidies for elder housing. We believe also that all poor people in this country should be able to live decently.

Many local governments will not undertake this responsibility. Representatives and activists among the younger poor and the older poor should get together to see that state and federal departments of housing, through HUD, should force this housing down the throats of local officials in cities, counties, townships and villages.

14

Elders: Time to Retire?

The age for mandatory retirement has now gone up to age seventy. It's a step forward. But it will not help the millions who are already retired. Very few of us will get back on company payrolls. We have the right to work. But we can't eat rights. Only those with special skills or unusual abilities will be rehired.

Our struggle to make ends meet will go on. So will our state of financial misery. Inflation will reduce the buying power of our Social Security and pension incomes. The already retired under age seventy are in the same bind as before the retirement age was extended.

But there is this difference. We can now, at least, be listed as "unemployed." We can make a stab at getting back on somebody's payroll. Between age sixty-five and seventy we occupy a special place in the job market. The unemployment statisticians will be forced to recognize this change in our status.

They will need to set up a new category for us. Census takers will need to ask, "Would you take a job if you could get one?" If the answer is "yes," we'll get listed among the jobless. We might also put on record our former job classification and income.

This won't be much help in getting a job, of course. It won't help pay the share of doctor's bills Medicare doesn't cover. Nor will it help us pay for prescription drugs or for dental help. It will, however, show how much the country is losing because our skills are not being utilized. Even that won't be much consolation. But it can add a new dimension to the planning and work of the CETA program.

CETA is the Comprehensive Employment and Training Act (Titles I, II and VI of the Older Americans Act). If this act were fairly administered, a great many of us could get back to work, on payrolls. Some of us would work part-time. Others would work full-time. But we would be making money. We would be living better. We would be happier.

CETA is a job assistance program which spends $12.1 billion a year. But at this time, according to the Labor Department, only 0.8 per cent of the 2.1 per cent of the elders who could be served benefit from the CETA expenditure. We are being blatantly discriminated against—officially.

The CETA administrators offer as an excuse for this discrimination the Title IX employment program. "The money for this is specifically earmarked for seniors," they say. What they don't say is that the Title IX funds are only $340 million. That's a drop in the bucket compared to the $12.1 *billion* allotted to CETA.

When this injustice is pointed out to CETA administrators, they fall back on another excuse. "Services to the young," they say, "assure more cost-to-benefit efficiency.

They produce a better return on the CETA investment." In a program developed for human needs, this is hardly a proper response.

Now comes Secretary of Labor Marshall to announce a two-hundred-man investigation of the entire CETA administration. The purpose is to "root out fraud, mismanagement and abuses" in the administration of the Comprehensive Employment and Training Act.

CETA has 750,000 people in its program. It is aimed at reducing unemployment. The amount of misused funds runs into the millions of dollars. "Every dollar that is wasted in the CETA program," Marshall declared, "is a dollar taken out of the pockets of the jobless." This includes the jobless under age seventy as well.

Marshall's investigators will also look into the political derring-do of the CETA administration. This affects us elders as badly as the mismanagement and discrimination. CETA is a political plum the size of a watermelon. All the local administrators are politically appointed.

Ditto all the heads of senior citizen offices. The result is obvious. If an elder is a Democrat in a Republican county, he's usually out of luck. And vice versa.

Yet, when we consider unemployed elders between age sixty-five and seventy, we come up with an odd fact. Most of us don't really *want* full-time jobs at full-time income. We don't want to get back into the rat race. We'd just like to add enough money to our take-home to ease the tight spot we're in. Making it on Social Security plus a small pension is uncomfortable for some. It is impossible for others.

Pin down the amount of extra money we'd like to make. Ask any older person to name a figure. He or she would probably come up with $4,000 yearly. Or he'd say, "Eighty dollars a week would ease our situation." That's the point at which Social Security starts taking fifty cents off every dollar we get in Social Security.

The $4,000 extra a year would be clear. And for a large number of us, it would be enough. We could pay medical bills which are not fully covered by Medicare. We could pay for medicines. We could buy eyeglasses. We could buy presents for the grandchildren. We could, in our own quiet ways, "live a little."

On this basis CETA could spread a great deal of cheer among us. We'd be trained for new jobs. We'd be retrained and so return to the firms we worked for in the past. Too many of us are not enjoying our retirement. We don't like being "has-beens." We need the comforts new income can pay for. We need, even more, the relationships to the "working" society from which we've been excluded. We need, most of all, the pride and the status employment assures in a work-oriented society.

CETA can either train us for part-time jobs or employ us on a part-time basis. It's a good bet that the majority of us will elect to be retrained. We will want re-employment in businesses or industries to the operations of which we once contributed.

Questions: Will the firms we worked for take us back? Will business and industry be willing or able to absorb us? Will our trade unions benefit by our return to work?

For the answer to these questions, we need to look at the employment policies of two types of firms, those who retire their workers at a specific age, and those who do not.

We will start with an example of one company which specifies no retirement age at all. It maintains the same policies toward its elderly employees as it does for younger employees.

A Louis Harris poll was quoted in *Forbes* magazine of July 1976 as follows: "More than half of those employees who are forcibly retired are bitter about it." Mr. Harris' polls have also shown that 61 per cent of those now working will be retired because of age—not ability. We who are already retired can attest to the truth of both these statements.

We present, therefore, the Bankers Life and Casualty Company, which has had, in its thirty years of growth, no problems in retaining its elderly employees. "Our experience," says Mr. John MacArthur, eighty-year-old founder of Bankers Life and Casualty, "has been consistently favorable throughout a variety of economic cycles and stages of company growth."

Mr. MacArthur continues, "Basically, our position is this. We maintain the same employment policies toward our elderly employees as we do toward all other 'identifiable' groups. All employees are expected to contribute their best efforts. They are expected to utilize their abilities to the extent called for by their position in the company."

At Bankers Life and Casualty, all three standard arguments advanced in favor of *forced* retirement have been proved false. Let's take them in the order of their importance.

"When older workers stay on the payroll, they prevent younger workers from moving up. They block the line of progression and cause young workers to leave."

It hasn't worked that way at Bankers Life Company. Growth, changes in organizational structure, job posting plans, employee counseling and training have worked to assure advancement to younger workers.

Consider the second unfair charge against older workers. "They are slow and forgetful. They are set in their ways. They are not creative."

Bankers Life has not found that to be true. Lack of creativity is not caused by longevity. Bankers Life expects all its workers to be creative. And they are. The company keeps its lines of communications open to all. Bankers Life has discovered a profound truth. When a young person forgets to do something, it's passed off as absentmindedness. When an older person forgets something, it's called senility.

The final criticism of the aged is "They hang in there even when they can no longer do the job."

The experience of Bankers Life and Casualty does not bear this out. When an older employee can no longer handle a job, the company considers him or her for other positions which are more appropriate. It doesn't retire the employee unless a suitable position cannot be found.

It turns out, also, that older employees are the first to realize that the job is suffering. They seek voluntary retirement. The decision is motivated by pride, regard for fellow or sister workers and regard for the company. Bankers Life and Casualty Company submits a breakdown in percentages of employees by age for the last twenty-five years. Here it is:

PERCENTAGE OF EMPLOYEES	OVER 50	OVER 55	OVER 60	OVER 65
1954	24%	15%	8%	Unknown
1968	27%	16%	7%	3%
1977	25%	17%	8%	4%

So much for the last argument in favor of forced retirement. The company has not grown top-heavy with older workers. At age sixty-five, treatment of each person as an individual has been a successful policy for Bankers Life and Casualty. The older people prove on the job, every working day of their lives, that they deserve the right to work.

Businesses generally, however, are worried. They see the retirement at age seventy law as another form of government interference. It is another challenge to the rights of corporations to operate without regard to social values. They resent the extended age of retirement because of the problems they foresee. To many, the new law is another step toward socialism.

What many businesses fail to understand is that the number of capable elders is increasing. The oldster of the 1980s is not a lost soul. His or her hand is not held out begging for consideration as a needy person. The statistics supplied by Bankers Life and Casualty bear this out.

Business and industry will have six months to comply with the new retirement at age seventy law. It will be illegal to force retirement before that age. The granting of pensions will not change this dictum. What options remain in this area of management?

The employer will no longer be the sole judge of the efficiency of his older employees who have become sixty-five years old. He will be forced to *prove* that they cannot do their jobs. They will be in a position to sue the firm which fires them.

In some departments of business, standards of performance measurements are now the rule. Business will not be permitted to change these measurements to force older workers to quit voluntarily. Nor will suddenly increased performance demands hold up in a court of law if the elder sues the company. If productivity as a whole can be proved by a worker or group of workers, the company may lose its case.

Therefore, systems for evaluating employees must develop specificity. Job descriptions must be precise. Unsatisfactory performers who have not been permitted a probationary period during which they can improve their output will have a legal case if fired. So, too, will those whose quality of work is doubtful.

Companies with generous pension plans are naturally in the best position to encourage early retirement of questionably productive workers. Such employees are generally indifferent to their work. Some hate their jobs. They won't do any better or more productive work during a probation period. They can be fired without fear of lawsuits.

There are companies whose management is ideologically locked into the age sixty-five retirement syndrome. They will need to raise their sights. They will find employees worth keeping on the job for as many more years as they can. These are the good workers. They are the ones who set examples to the young. They take pride in their work. They are satisfied that the company is a good company for which to work.

Such personnel are valuable. The efforts of personnel departments should be to encourage them to stay on until age seventy and beyond. What's involved here is not obedience to the laws of profit. These are exactly the people who will quit voluntarily when they no longer meet the challenges of their jobs.

Trade unions which administer pension plans favor the age seventy retirement law for reasons of their own. Five more years at work produce five more years of dues. At the same time, they produce five fewer years when the unions are required to pay out pensions. The interest and dividends in the pension fund grow.

American industry will adjust to the age seventy retirement laws. It adjusted to government rules that insisted it open jobs for blacks and other minorities. It adjusted to government rules changing policies related to the hiring of women. Now the government has granted workers five more years on the job. Industry will adjust to these rules too.

Back in Germany, in 1889, Prince Otto von Bismarck established the world's first pension plan. German workers were to go on pensions at age sixty-five. Workers contributed to the pension fund. Employers contributed to the pension fund. The only difference between Bismarck's program and ours here was that the German government added to the pension from the German National Treasury.

But that was back in 1889. Very few workers *lived* to age sixty-five. The costs to industry and to the German treasury were minimal. The workers who lived to age sixty-five paid of course. They weren't around long enough to get their money back.

It's a different world now. A majority of Americans do live to a ripe old age. What is more, they remain valid throughout their lives. When American companies realize this, their entire attitude toward elders will change. A good older worker will be rated by the way he does his job.

That will be the time when age will no longer be a criterion for hiring or passing up a good worker on a part- or full-time basis. May that time *begin* with the age seventy retirement law. May it prove that there's no reason to fire any worker at any age.

15

Third Interlude

Every writer needs a wife like Nikka. Her understanding of sentence structure is positively uncanny. Her sense of the precisely fitting word and the form of expression within the sentence is equally remarkable.

When I concoct an awkward phrase, she challenges it. Of course, she's gentle about it. But she's firm. She's usually right. So I rewrite. The truth is I've given up checking my thesaurus. Sheer laziness.

There weren't too many "awkwardities" in the two chapters on Homemaker Home Health Aide services. Mostly those chapters were reportorial. Nikka read the chapters. She suggested a few changes which I accepted. But she seemed reluctant to return the manuscript to me.

"Something wrong?" I asked.

"I'm a little lost," she answered.

"What do you mean lost?"

"Your data are probably accurate. At least, I'm in no position to challenge you. But there's no real *fight* in your conclusions for these two chapters."

I was a little miffed at that. "Are you saying that I ought to scream a little louder?"

She flipped the pages of the two chapters. "Screaming won't help either chapter," she said thoughtfully. "They sort of hang in the middle distance. These are weak chapters. They don't go anywhere."

"Well," I rejoined, "do you disagree with my conclusions?"

"They don't go far enough. There's no solid resolution in either chapter. Granted that the sense of continuity of the two chapters makes it unnecessary for you to wind things up at the end of the *first* chapter. But there are no specific recommendations at the end of the second chapter either. Something's missing but I can't put my finger on just what it is."

She returned the manuscript to me without further comment. I took it up to my office. (That was formerly our son Jonathan's bedroom.) Then she went into her study. (That was formerly our daughter Heather's bedroom.) Sometimes Nikka turns her study into a sewing room. She is deep into patchwork quilts and other needle-and-thread-type handicraft projects.

I reread the chapters. I had learned over our lifetime not to take Nikka's comments lightly. To be sure, this criticism was vague enough. But she obviously felt that something was missing in the chapters on Homemaker Home Health Aide.

I had to find out what was wrong. The problems as presented were, as she said, "unresolved." I had to determine where I had missed the boat.

Well, I read the two chapters three times. You, dear reader, have read them too (I hope). Obviously, this wasn't simply a matter of editing. I knew that a rewrite wouldn't change the essential interpretation of the data significantly. The facts were all there. They had been correctly analyzed. In terms of the book's drive toward activism by elders for elders little seemed to be missing.

Finally, as you'd expect, Nikka spotted the weakness. I walked into her study, which was at the time a sewing room. The machine was rattling along noisily. I said, somewhat belligerently, "I can't find anything wrong with these chapters."

"I've been thinking about them, too," she replied. "Take a look at your wind-up of your second chapter on home health. Read it out loud to me."

I did.

"Reread please, the bombast in the final line which says, 'This is a battle we can win!' That's pure hogwash."

"The hell it is! If we elders take leadership as the previous paragraph says, we *can* win on this one."

"And just *what* can we win? Be more specific."

"A national workable Homemaker Home Health Aide program. That's what we can win."

"Nothing in what you wrote in these chapters leads to such a conclusion. You can't wish these changes into existence. You haven't clarified the 'how.' You haven't even explained what a 'workable' program is."

Nikka turned back to her sewing. I marched disconsolately back to my office. She was right, of course. I had no right to expect every reader to agree with me. That would be arrogant. But I did owe it to readers to sum up the various key factors that relate to in-home health services.

I knew that I'd covered the general medical situation of elders in chapter 3 of this book. That chapter concerned the reluctance of doctors to treat us. It also explained that practitioners in "family medicine" might provide some help to the aging.

Family medicine doctors would learn about our conditions because in family medicine so many of us elders would be under their care.

Now it was time for a chapter which brought together our whole medical situation as it concerned us elders.

Nikka had finished her work. Her sewing room was once more to be a study. I helped her shove the sewing machine back to its place against the wall under her bookshelves.

"What would you say," I asked, "if I wrote a summary chapter on health for the aged?"

"You said it. I didn't."

"But you do remember, Nik, that way back in chapter 3 I laid out some of our medical problems. Will readers go back to reread that chapter? What happens to sequence?"

"It's your book, isn't it? You can move chapter 3 forward or move the home health stuff back. My guess is that readers will remember chapter 3. Or they'll check back on it to refresh their thinking."

Well, readers, I left chapter 3 where it was. I make no apologies for that. Excuse the interruption of this interlude. Just read on.

16

Elders: In-Home Health Care

We square our aged shoulders. We plunge headlong into the morass of medical and health care and homemaking services for elders. Different areas of the country, different political jurisdictions approach our health problems in different ways.

First, therefore, let's understand what health care and medical services are supposed to do for us. We state these objectives simply.

If we're well and in good health: The medical and health care services should help us to stay that way. That could be a matter of health education which would teach us to take better care of ourselves. Such education would be administered locally. Schools, colleges, hospitals and social services, organizations like the Red Cross would also help.

If we're sick: Professional health care should prevent us from getting sicker. Such a program would be aimed at curing temporary illness or controlling chronic ailments.

If we're bedridden: In-home medical and supportive social services should be available. Local medical and professional nursing and social services should include *outreach*. The assessment of the specific needs should be made by a physician and a member of the Social Services Department.

If we require medical treatment but are not bedridden: Day hospitals should be established throughout the country. That way elders can be brought to the hospital, be treated there one or more days a week. They could *go home* after each treatment is administered. (Note: A day hospital is not a clinic.)

When we need prescription medication: It should be free for all recipients of Medicare and Medicaid. As of now, only Medicaid recipients receive free drugs.

What we elders are up against is this. Effective treatment programs for every situation described above do exist in individual communities *somewhere* in the United States. Our struggle must be to see to it that *all* the effective treatments should be available *everywhere* in the United States.

Look at it this way. Social Security and Medicare are the *only* federal projects for elders which provide federal money directly from Washington. Medicaid policies vary from state to state. One state, in fact, doesn't even have a Medicaid program. That's Arizona.

Medicare has two parts—hospital insurance and medical insurance. Hospital insurance helps pay for inpatient hospital care and post-hospital care in a skilled nursing facility or in-home care from a home health aide agency. Medical insurance helps pay doctor bills and other services not covered by hospital insurance.

Medicaid pays the full costs of these and other health care services for those eligible.

Medicare hospital insurance is financed by payroll contributions from employers and employees. Medical insurance is financed with premiums. Those enrolled pay about 30 per cent of the cost. The federal government pays the remainder.

Medicaid is financed by federal and state governments. The federal share ranges from 50 per cent for the richest states up to 73 per cent for the states with the lower per-capita income. States pay the remaining costs, often with help from local governments.

(For the record: You call your local Social Security office for information about Medicare. You call your local Department of Social Services for information about Medicaid.)

Consider this also. Many hospitals over the country have clubs for ex-patients. These include heart clubs, diabetes clubs, stroke clubs and clubs for other long-term ailments or catastrophic attacks. The fellowship with other elders facing identical problems is wonderfully reassuring. It is our job as elders to see that our own local hospitals have such clubs.

Essentially, these clubs are educational. They provide post-factum assistance. People learn to live with their disabilities.

Now at Nassau Community Hospital in Oceanside, New York, Dr. Martin Posner, Director of Community Medicine, comes up with an educational program called PATH. The acronym stands for People Activated Towards Health. PATH advances the *educational* theme for elders several steps.

On June 17, 1978, PATH graduated twenty-nine men and women in an impressive ceremony. PATH certificates were given to twenty-nine men and women, *retirees* if you please. They ranged from age fifty-five to eighty-three. These volunteers had equipped themselves to spot chronic disease symptoms. They also became certified cardiopulmonary resuscitation practitioners (CPRs).

Dr. Posner's course consisted of thirty-one lessons. It took three months of serious study by participants to complete the course. The elderly volunteers learned about the signs and symptoms of dysfunction. A few reports of the PATH courses follow:

Lesson 8 covers the digestive system. The focus is on signs and symptoms of dysfunction. There's an introduction to the Hemoccult, a test kit used to screen occult (unrecognized) blood in the stool. The appearance of such blood may be an early sign of cancer in the large bowel.

Lesson 15 provides an introduction to laboratory diagnostics. Students get to understand the workings of CAT-scanners, ultrasonics, nuclear medicine, xerography, etc. Remember we're talking about retirees.

PATH graduates, volunteers all, now know what constitutes a complete medical examination. They get a basic understanding of the circulatory system, its anatomy and its physiology, along with some discussion of the pathology involving this system.

Lesson 29 deals with the upper respiratory tract: signs and symptoms of specific diseases and how to recognize them. Lesson 30 explains the central nervous system.

We come to Lesson 31. That's a very practical money matter. The volunteers understand health reimbursement mechanisms. They learn about the Patients' Bill of Rights and how to define "informed consent."

Now we ask, "Why cannot elders in other parts of the

country work to get PATH and other educational programs started in their local hospitals?"

We cite PATH as an example. If we elders want to improve medical care education in our own communities, we will have to start the job and do the job *ourselves*. And that includes the task of *educating ourselves* first.

We elders have important responsibilities to brother and sister seniors. Take the health situation of the *urban* aged. Among them we find isolated, homebound, abandoned elders. These people rate as the medically "unreached."

Now, so far as we can learn, there are only two, repeat only two, hospital *outreach* programs to serve these unfortunate elders. Their problems are complex and multi-faceted. Physical disabilities, disorientation and psychological disorders are only part of the problem. The basic need is to combat situations which include poor housing, no money and social isolation.

We will give you, first of all, the names and addresses of the hospitals now working actively in this area of outreach. In New York, the Chelsea-Village Program (Greenwich Village), Philip W. Brickner, M.D., Director. Address: St. Vincent's Hospital, 153 West 11th Street, New York, N.Y. 10011. Phone: (212) 790-8063.

In Chicago it's the Five Hospitals Homebound Elderly Program, Evelyn M. McNamara, Director. Address: 501 Surf Street, Chicago, Ill. 60657. Phone: (312) 549-5822.

Do you know why we're giving you these names and addresses? We expect readers who live in urban communities to write for further information about these projects. When the information comes through, we expect them to get together with other elders and to start a drive for effective hospital outreach through local hospitals. Form a committee and get to work.

The Chelsea-Village Program began January 18, 1973. It provided professional health services for homebound, isolated, abandoned aged people. The initiative came from St. Vincent's Hospital Medical Center of New York and the Chelsea and Greenwich Village communities.

The program started in a small way with St. Vincent's professional hospital staff and no money. Dr. Brickner knew that reimbursement by Medicaid and Medicare would not be forthcoming. (Hospitals may not bill for care outside the institutions. Our fight here is to change that rule.)

At the start, organizers of the Chelsea-Village Program included two physicians, a social worker and a nurse. The first group to be served was residents of "welfare hotels." The organizing group established a clinic in the largest of these hotels.

Dr. Brickner reports: "The derelicts involved were too indifferent, frightened or angry to seek needed health care through local hospitals or physicians. These were men and women who would rather die in the hotel than make the effort to get treatment elsewhere. They were put off by the regimentation of the hospitals.

"We learned also that badly damaged as these men and women were by their sociopathic behavior, the *older* people among them were the worst off. They suffered the combined burdens of a deteriorated style of life and the physical consequences of aging.

"Based on this understanding, we took another look at our own community and realized that aged people, particularly those who were homebound and alone, were a medically unreached group. We can say of the first group—al-

coholic derelict men—that they *will* not participate in the
health care system. We can equally well say of homebound
aged people that they *cannot*. They are barred from the system by their own disabilities."

We are not here going to tell the whole success story.
From the beginning, the initiators of the program spoke to
representatives of every community agency in the two districts. These included, as Dr. Brickner reports further:
". . . all three police precincts; the two settlement houses
in our area; fire stations; the offices of the three congressmen
whose districts merge here; city and state politicians; Office
of Economic Opportunity programs; senior citizens centers;
every church and synagogue; local planning boards; block
associations. We found a universal understanding of the
need and willingness to help."

Dr. Brickner continues, "We approached our hospital administrators at a time when financial stress upon the voluntary hospital system in New York City was severe and getting worse. Administration's reaction was favorable, and to
the present time the hospital continues its support. It takes
an unusual administration to recognize the imperatives of
this kind of program. The response from the Sisters of Charity of St. Vincent de Paul who run St. Vincent's Hospital is a
realistic application of the founding spirit of that institution.
It was created in 1849 to care for the sick poor.

"We had well-attended group meetings with hospital and
community representatives. These sessions served to introduce our ideas widely through the hospital and through our
geographic area. They resulted in agreements with other
voluntary and governmental agencies to participate in care
of our patients, and helped to create the atmosphere of in-

terest and expectation necessary for finding of these hidden patients."

As to statistics of the area to be covered: Chelsea has about 85,000 residents of mixed ethnic background. Greenwich Village has 75,000 people split among both economic and ethnic lines. The basic program was aimed at helping patients to remain in their own homes and community, keeping them out of institutions in the best possible state of health and with maximum independence.

Early cases proved the viability of Dr. Brickner's concept. In that period of the activity, the big questions were "Will the program produce sufficient referrals? Is anybody paying attention?" Dr. Brickner and his staff need not have worried.

Referrals came from many local sources. Within a month the program had more cases than they could handle. The project as of January 1978 reported 589 patients: 376 women, 213 men.

It is interesting to note that of the total, 546 patients were over sixty, 39 were between ninety and ninety-nine; 2 were one hundred years old plus.

As this is being written, Appleton-Century-Crofts announces the publication of a book by Dr. Brickner, *Home Health Care for the Aged.*

Chicago's joint cooperative outreach project, Five Hospitals Homebound Elderly Program (FHHEP), involves Augustine, Columbus, Grant, Illinois Masonic and St. Joseph hospitals.

The administrators of these five hospitals pledged $7,000 each to fund the first year of operation. The Mayor's Office for Senior Citizens provided a grant of $15,000 to help fund FHHEP. According to the 1970 census the Lincoln Park-

Lakeview area of Chicago is the most densely concentrated area of senior citizens (sixty-five and over) of any neighborhood in the city of Chicago.

The program has the following objectives:

1. To provide comprehensive, coordinated medical and social supportive services primarily to the homebound elderly. To develop a team approach to the delivery of care to the homebound elderly which would include the services of a physician and a cadre of health care and social service supportive personnel.

2. To provide all services required to maintain those older adults who wish to remain in their own home. To work cooperatively with existing health and social services in the community to meet the needs of the homebound elderly and to avoid duplication of efforts and services.

3. To identify gaps in resources, services and financing mechanisms which prevent chronically ill older adults from remaining in their homes and to work cooperatively with community agencies to eliminate those gaps. To train health care personnel in the specialized needs and problems of the older adult and to create new manpower resources where necessary to fulfill these needs.

4. To reduce the number of emergency and repeated hospitalizations which have been the primary means for many elderly to receive medical care. To create new opportunities of employment and volunteer service for the older adult.

5. To demonstrate through careful program evaluation that a comprehensive and coordinated program of medical and supportive services can reduce the need for premature or inappropriate institutionalization of the elderly.

6. To determine if home maintenance can be a more cost-

effective and efficient way of caring for large numbers of elderly than institutionalization.

The program will provide service on a priority basis to:

1. Homebound persons who live alone, or with another dependent individual and who are not presently under regular physician or hospital care.

2. Persons receiving physician or hospital care and in need of a variety of in-home supportive services in order to be maintained outside of an institution.

3. Chronically ill dependent persons under sixty, who are alone or who live with another dependent individual and have similar needs.

We now ask direct questions. Why does not Medicare or Medicaid cover the costs of hospital outreach services to elders? The programs conducted by the five hospitals in Chicago and by the Chelsea-Village activity in New York are obviously important and beneficial to seniors. The trouble is that at this time few hospitals can *afford* to provide this service. Neither Medicare nor Medicaid pays for it.

This calls for a concerted effort by elders *actively* to go to bat for a change in Medicare/Medicaid rules. We have our two national organizations of seniors—the National Council of Senior Citizens (NCSC), and the American Association of Retired Persons and National Retired Teachers Association (AARP/NRTA). We have state and local organizations. Outreach by hospitals has proved itself in two urban areas.

Our responsibility as activist elders and the responsibility of our local and national organizations are clear. We should put the pressure on Medicare and Medicaid to change their rules. Hospital outreach should be one of the services for which Medicare and Medicaid pay. It is unseemly for hospitals to be forced to seek financial support from private philanthropy and community agencies for this important outreach to medically unreached seniors.

At this point, we switch our emphasis from outreach to intake, which is the purpose of day hospitals. This too is a health idea for seniors which needs as big a push by activist elders as do the outreach projects so far discussed.

A day hospital is called a day hospital because elders visit the hospital several days a week for treatment. They can even get into a bed while there at the hospital.

These patients go home at night.

The American Hospital Association keeps no records on day hospitals and can supply no information about how many hospitals operate day programs in the United States. But it is obvious that day hospitals can keep elders out of nursing homes.

Our first contact with day hospitals was in England. We'll describe the operation of Withington Hospital, run by the Department of Geriatric Medicine in Manchester, England, quoting from their leaflet for patients and relatives.

"It is called a Day Hospital because you spend most of the daytime there, for one, two or three days a week, but you sleep at home as usual. The Day Hospital is meant for elderly people who have some disease such as a stroke, or arthritis, or other complaint which can be helped by treatment.

"The Day Hospital has nurses and doctors who will look after the medical side of your case. But there are also physiotherapists who will try to build up your strength and improve your walking and balance. If you have difficulty with speech, or making yourself understood, you can be given help by the Speech Therapists. There is also a Dietitian, who will advise you about special diets and food in general.

"You may be having difficulty with things like dressing, getting on and off the toilet, getting out of a chair, cooking, and other everyday things. The Day Hospital has experts who will help you with this.

"If you have problems about money, your house care or things of that kind, there are medical social workers to advise you."

We call your special attention to the last paragraph of Withington Hospital's leaflet. It is a tip-off. Great Britain has a national health program. In this country, the Kennedy-Corman bill for a national health plan has been kicking around for years. The bills are House of Representatives H.R. 21, U.S. Senate S3. President Carter has promised us a national health plan as well. But that has now been put off, too. Nothing in the propaganda on national health plans discusses home health and medical services as they operate in Great Britain.

Day hospitals in that country are backed up by a network of home helpers. Teams of social service workers, which include nursing care where needed, carry the ball from the day hospital to the home. The day hospital patients throughout Great Britain get home to a clean house, to a hot evening meal and chore services across the board.

Two day hospitals have recently been established on Long Island. These are St. Francis Hospital in Roslyn and the Jewish Institute for Geriatric Care in New Hyde Park. My own limited research on day hospitals in the United States produces the names of Peninsula General Hospital in Far Rockaway and the Geriatric Day Center at Montefiore Hospital in New York.

There are also the Baptist Church Hospital in Warwick, Rhode Island; the Burke Rehabilitation Center in White Plains, New York; St. Camillus Nursing Home in Syracuse, New York; and Metropolitan Jewish Geriatric Center in Brooklyn, New York.

There are, of course, other day care hospitals scattered about the country. But they are few and far between. Even the American Hospital Association can't supply a list.

We have offered in three chapters a canvas of alternatives to institutionalization in nursing homes. We have proved that day hospitals and in-home health care, plus supportive social services, are less costly than nursing home care. Together these three activities will reduce the number of elders who will be suffering indignities in nursing homes.

It is now time to summarize what activist elders can do to assure independent living in their own homes for themselves and for brother and sister elders.

On a federal level our task is to force the Department of Health, Education and Welfare to set up guidelines. These would be backed by strict rules and regulations. Both profit and non-profit services in home health care in all states would be required to conform to these regulations. The penalty for non-conformance would be reduction of financial help to the states.

On state and local levels, our task would be to set up organizations which would police the in-home health nursing and homemaker companies.

The effort would be to remove the licenses of those who were ripping off the government or gouging the recipients of the services and the state's money.

We should be pushing for a national and/or state accreditation system such as that set up by independent consumer organizations. The National Council for Homemaker Home Health Aide, Inc. has set up standards both for accreditation and quality of service. Our organizations of elders should work closely with such groups.

The address of the National Council for Homemaker Home Health Aide, Inc. is 67 Irving Place, New York, N.Y. 10003. Telephone: (212) 674-4990.

Let's face this basic fact. At our age, any one of us may have a need for in-home health services. If we organize and take a hand in the struggle to keep in-home health companies honest and effective, we will stay out of nursing homes.

17

Elders: Handicapped

We reach our sixties. Physical disabilities plague us. Few of us are entirely whole.

The medical profession keeps us going. Pharmacists supply pills and nostrums. Our arthritis or gout, or vertigo or heart conditions or flatulence, may not be curable. They are kept in suspension. But we manage to live in spite of disabilities of this kind. In the process of growing old, some parts of us function less effectively than others. We cope with all of our lesser and some of our major difficulties.

This should comfort us average elders. It is a personal conquest over our various disabilities. We get accustomed to aches and pains. Many of us have survived major illnesses during our lifetimes. We became reconciled to the "hangovers" resulting from these attacks. We live cautiously.

The truth is, also, that we aren't particularly envious of the number of "heroes" among us. They brag too much. They're still playing tennis at age sixty-four? How nice for them. They jog their five miles a day? We pretend we're impressed. They play eighteen or thirty-six holes of golf twice a week? Ho-hum.

Disabilities can be rated by degrees. They go from minor, to partial, to hypochondria. However, there is a qualitative difference between having a disability and living with a handicap. A disability is a matter of personal adjustment. A handicap is not.

A wheelchair can't climb steps. A sightless person can't cross a street with ease. How does a person who uses a "walker" get into a toilet of standard dimensions?

Figuratively speaking, there's always a boy scout around to cross us over to the opposite side of the street. We may not need or want to get there. But along with others, a boy scout sees a gray-haired person as helpless. Who among us elders will deny the scout his merit badge? Which one of us will refuse to a kindly person the pleasure of "doing something" for the elderly?

Yes. We elders with disabilities tend to accept the condescension of the young. They mean well. Sometimes, indeed, their assistance is valuable.

But the handicapped among us have special problems. Their struggle is with the environment in which they are forced to live. Even in simple situations they face insurmountable barriers. They need a different and higher level of assistance from all sectors of society and especially from our government.

First, let's review some statistics. Urban Institute statistics for the year 1975 revealed the following:

- As of 1975, one fourth of Americans sixty-five and older were either disabled or handicapped.

- In other age groups, 23.3 million adults between ages eighteen and sixty-four were disabled or handicapped.
- An additional 2 million persons were disabled and institutionalized.
- Eight million young people between ages three and twenty-one were disabled enough to require special education in public schools.
- Another million handicapped children of school age were not in school at all.

These figures argue that solving the problems of disabled and handicapped Americans is a valid national issue of major proportions. They also confirm the necessity for elder activists to take leadership in efforts to help their contemporaries who are disabled or handicapped.

Elders and their families should concern themselves with the issue for two reasons. Too many Americans consider age itself a barrier to full participation in the life of their communities. A number of us may, at any time, find ourselves physically incapable of such participation. Our social and other activities are always at risk. The hale and hearty elders of today may become the elder incapacitatees of tomorrow.

When we grow old our senses, motor responses, attitudes and emotional behavior undergo changes. There is visual loss. There is auditory loss. There are disorientations of various kinds. We need to look to architects who will design safe, comfortable and non-frustrating environments for elders and other impaired people.

We also need to be aware that in this country, government officials and volunteer groups are prepared, even anxious, to help us. Manufacturers have designed products and devices which offset losses due to physical impairments.

There's a non-profit organization in New York called the American Standards Institute (ASI). Its purpose is to set up specifications for making buildings and facilities accessible to, and usable by, the physically handicapped.

Fifty-one organizations approve and subscribe to the ASI objectives. These organizations range from the AFL-CIO to the American Society of Landscape Architects. They include the American Institute of Architects and the American Society of Mechanical Engineers. Government administrations involved with housing, health and welfare, education and labor also work with the American Standards Institute. As far back as 1956, President Eisenhower set up the President's Committee on Employment of the Physically Handicapped. He called a general conference of groups interested in this problem.

In 1961, the American Standards Institute came through with specifications for the manufacture and building of facilities and equipment used by the disabled and handicapped. These began with specifications for wheelchairs and their functioning. They moved from the grading of sites at developments, to walks, parking lots, buildings, doors and doorways, stairs, floors, toilet rooms, telephone booths, elevator controls. The ASI provided also a list of hazards faced by the physically impaired.

The national standards specifications were reaffirmed in 1971. At this writing they are being updated to take advantage of new expertise, new construction and new manufacturing techniques developed since the 1971 standards were set up.

In Washington, the Architectural and Transportation Bar-

riers Compliance Board came into being. It was created by
Congress in 1973. The primary objective of the Compliance
Board was to see to it that all buildings and facilities owned,
financially supported and occupied by the U. S. Government
be accessible to and usable by handicapped persons.

The Architectural Barriers Act of 1968 (Public Law
90-480) pinned the rules down. Beginning on August 12,
1968, "All government buildings designed, constructed, altered or leased by the Federal government and supported
financially, wholly or in part with Federal funds *must be
barrier-free.*"

The Compliance Board is composed of Cabinet-level representatives from nine federal departments and agencies.
These include the Departments of Health, Education and
Welfare; Housing and Urban Development; Labor; Interior;
Defense. They also include the General Service Administration, the U. S. Postal Service and the Veterans Administration.

An impressive list of important government people, right?
Why then should the Compliance Board be satisfied to eliminate barriers in government buildings only? We elders need
to ask, "What are they doing to spread and promote the use
of the American Standards Institute's specifications *nationally?* Which states, which cities, which areas of the country
have passed laws or regulations to eliminate barriers for the
disabled or handicapped?"

We have among us elders people who are orthopedically
or neurologically handicapped. We know that there are
blind people and deaf people and people who must use walkers and crutches and wheelchairs. All are shut out by architectural barriers from the world and from the work and associations they formerly enjoyed.

Moreover, elders especially are subject to *attitudinal* barriers. These are based on distaste, or stereotyping, or fear, or ignorance. We struggle constantly against ideological put-downs as well as physical barriers.

It's a toss-up. Which of the two types of barriers is more onerous? The cliché attitudes exist because we are old. The physical barriers exist because we have in some ways become incapacitated. The situation is grim.

Let's suppose that even a few of the physical barriers are removed. Curbs are cut. Ramps are built alongside staircases. Doors are widened to supplement revolving doors with additional and wider entrances to buildings. Could not the disabled resume normal functions like the rest of society?

Not entirely. Disabled elders would still find it necessary to struggle for complete acceptance as valid citizens. People with psychological hang-ups would still shun the handicapped. Our ways of locomotion are too plainly seen. Wheelchairs, Seeing Eye dogs, braces, hearing aids induce feelings of fear and distrust among many Americans. Buildings, after all, are designed only for the physically fit. Elders and others with disabilities and handicaps would still remain frustrated, second-class citizens.

Jobs in offices or factories would still be closed to them. So would admissions to many schools and colleges. They couldn't use public accommodations and transportation. Simple acts like going to the store or movies would still be complicated for them.

The barriers they face are many. Narrow doors are closed doors to people in wheelchairs and those on crutches. Steps with or without side rails are impossible to climb. Revolving doors stop them cold. Ramps, where they exist, are often too steep and quite as often lead to doors which are too narrow. We ask again, "How does a person with a walker get into a toilet of standard dimensions?"

Conveniences which non-handicapped people take for granted are inconvenient for the incapacitated. Phone booths are too small. Bus steps are too high. Mirrors in public restrooms ditto. And how does a person in a wheelchair take a drink at a water fountain?

Many organizations work for the handicapped. The funds they raise are usually for research and rehabilitation. From research come programs.

Here we have, for example, the Industrial Home for the Blind (IHB) setting up a training program for professional and paraprofessional staffs in nursing homes. It is a formal program for eight hours of "continuation education." In New York State credits are granted by the Board of Examiners of Nursing Home Administrators.

The program covers first the physical and psychological aspects of blindness. It stresses the trauma of admission to a nursing home. Blindness may result in loss of dignity, self-sufficiency, privacy, decision making because of the new and unfamiliar surroundings. These may immobilize a blind person to the point that a diagnosis of "chronic brain syndrome" may be made because the blind person is not assisted to adjust.

Subsequent two-hour sessions cover "Orientation and Mobility Instruction for Blind Persons," "Skills for Daily Living" and "Participation in Recreational Activities."

Other educational programs promoted by the Industrial Home for the Blind teach domestic science (the kitchen or dining area) and, of course, "Safety." These become guides for counselors and other professionals in the field of the aging as well as for those who work with younger blind people.

A third educational aspect of the work of the IHB advises nurses and the general public on how to deal with blind persons. Two IHB booklets will serve as examples.

Here are instructions from a booklet for the general public entitled *When You Meet a Blind Person*. Study them carefully.

"When you see a blind person waiting to cross the street, ask if he needs your assistance. If he does, let him hold your arm. And make sure to walk all the way across with him.

"Speak directly to him, using a normal tone of voice. He won't mind words like 'see' or 'blind,' so you needn't censor your conversation.

"If he asks directions, be specific as to distance. It is useless, remember, to point or give visual landmarks. If he must make a turn, tell him whether it should be left or right.

"Assisting a blind person at stairs, guide his hand to the banister. At an escalator, tell him whether it is going up or down, then guide his hand to the moving rail just before he steps on.

"Entering a bus, walk ahead, keeping one step in front. Once inside, guide his hand to some support so he can steady himself.

"At a revolving door, let him go ahead of you. Guide his hand to the rubber flange on the edge of the door. And remind him to step to his right when he has gone through the door.

"Helping a blind person into a car, guide his hand to its roof—just over the door—if the door is open. If it is closed, place his hand on its handle. Make sure his hand is safely inside the car before you close the door.

"When accompanying a blind person into a room unfamiliar to him, never leave him standing alone in the middle of the floor. Escort him to a seat, or place his hand on a 'point of reference' such as a wall or table.

"Showing him to a chair, place his hand on its back or arm. He will seat himself.

"Speak when you enter a blind person's room. Identify yourself. When you are leaving the room, let him know.

"Changing money for a blind person, hand him each bill of a given denomination, telling him what it is. He can separate coins for himself.

"A guide dog walks on the blind person's left, so you should walk on his right. Don't distract the dog by petting it."

Another booklet, *When Your Patient Is Blind*, provides guidance for nurses. The theme in the nurses' booklet is "Guessing games are no fun if one person is not playing by choice."

The booklet begins, "Tell him what you're doing, who you are, what is on his tray, when you are going to touch him, what is in his room, what you're giving him.

"When you take a blind person somewhere, don't push, don't pull. Let him hold your arm, then he's half a step behind you. He will know when you stop or turn or step up or step down."

We elders must keep in mind the fact that any one of us may become handicapped; therefore, activist national and local organizations of elders must become more aware of this. Committees within our organizations set up to help the elderly handicapped will work two ways. They will increase membership and they will assure greater support for our cause.

Another example is necessary to prove this point. In August 1977, the Human Resources Center (HRC) at Albertson, Long Island, announced the establishment of a National Center on Employment of the Handicapped. Some background follows:

Back in 1952, a division of the HRC called Abilities, Inc. was started by a handicapped man named Henry Viscardi. At the time, Abilities, Inc. had a total work force of four disabled individuals. The company set out "to create an environment which would demonstrate the capabilities and productivity of disabled workers." More than four thousand handicapped workers have been employed by Abilities, Inc. over the years since 1952. The corporation is now deeply and profitably involved in such industries as telecommunications, data processing and electronics.

From this beginning, the Human Resources Center, a non-profit organization, came into being and developed a broad spectrum of programs for the handicapped. It has by now achieved international recognition by those working for handicapped people of all ages. The HRC offers a work "demonstration." This includes job training and placement, academic and vocational education. Independent living for the handicapped is the goal of all these programs.

Now our working years have been extended to age seventy. We elders who retire at sixty-five or earlier need jobs. We need to supplement our meager Social Security. Should we not, individually and organizationally, consider the HRC as a resource for re-establishing and updating our skills so that we can get part- or full-time jobs? Should we not make an effort to prove that age need *not* be a handicap?

Again we call on organizations of elders to form committees to investigate this area of opportunity. The first step would be to write for further information to: Human Resources Center, Albertson, Long Island, N.Y. 11507.

Keep in mind that every state in the union has a vocational rehabilitation center. Your local or state committees working for elders should, as a second step, visit these centers for local and state information.

Every state in the union also has an Easter Seal Society for Crippled Children and Adults which provides catalogs listing literature on handicapped and guide books to accessible facilities on a local basis.

This chapter on handicaps, like the earlier chapters of the book, insists that we elders must lead the fight for our own interests. No one will carry the battle for us.

We want to end barriers for the handicapped among us. We must, therefore, study and understand local building code rules. If we want the building or other codes enforced, we must confront local town boards or county and state officials and demand enforcement action.

If we want the services and the educational efforts of nonprofit "helping groups" to work for us, we must encourage them to bring their good deeds to us where we live.

If we are not for ourselves, ask the sages, who will be for us?

18

Elders: Volunteerism

You're a thoughtful, articulate, active elder. You play a part in a program which you know is important. Not to you personally. The project in which you are engaged helps other elders who are less fortunate than you. Or you could be performing a very useful service for children. No matter.

You tell middlescent people about what you do and how you are handling a specific situation. They say with some indifference and utmost condescension, "How nice. It keeps you busy."

The response brings you back to your childhood. Toward the end of every term your teachers had exam papers to mark. Or they had clerical tasks to perform. They cooked up what was known in the teaching trade as "busywork." Usually it was boring and useless. But it kept you out of mischief. Except for the liveliest kids in the class, nobody threw spitballs.

The expression "It keeps you busy" is without question

the most frequently used put-down we activist elders experience. The implication is totally negative. It assumes that nothing we do is useful or significant.

Of course, activist elders know how this supercilious attitude developed as it involved volunteers. In our society, the making of money is the be-all and end-all of activity. Too many of us grow up believing that "If you don't get paid for everything you do, it isn't worth doing at all."

As a result, elders of our generation are divided into two distinctly opposite groups. There are those who spend their retirement years playing games. They present their position philosophically. "We've paid our dues. Now we want to have a good time . . . fun, fun, fun."

A second, and unfortunately, a smaller sector of the elder population insists that a total involvement in fun and games is not enough to preserve their validity. Their philosophy expresses itself in what may justly be called "living by the golden rule."

It isn't that they spend *all* their time working for or with others. They too play and enjoy games and other leisure activities. But they choose from the multi-faceted opportunities to help or to serve others. They spend anywhere from several hours a day to several days a week working in projects which interest them.

They become volunteers.

How many elder volunteers are there? A study prepared for the National Council on the Aging (NCOA) by Louis Harris and Associates, Inc. submits the following figures. They appear on pages 94 and 95 of a report entitled *The Myth and Reality of Aging in America,*" published in January 1976.

Apart from any work they're paid for, 22% of the public 65 and older report that they do volunteer work.

Among those aged 65 to 69, 28% do volunteer work. Among older people with incomes of $7,000 or more, one elder in three said they do volunteer work.

Forty-two per cent of the older college-educated seniors do volunteer work.

Volunteerism is somewhat higher among older whites (23%) than among older blacks (15%). (Note: That's understandable. Blacks are usually on the receiving end of assistance.)

A higher proportion of employed people 65 and older (33%) than those not employed (20%) do volunteer work.

The percentage breakdown of volunteers from age 55 and older reads as follows: 55 to 64, 33%; 65 to 69, 28%; 70 to 79, 20%; 80 and older, 12%.

As of 1975, there were 22 million of us elders. We constituted 13 per cent of the population of the United States, which totaled 212 million at that time. Twenty-two per cent or 4.8 million elders are volunteers. Reduce the number by the 5 per cent of elders who are institutionalized. You come out with a grand total of 3.7 million effective elder volunteers.

We have a perfect right to be proud of ourselves. But we can't rest on our laurels. We need to convince brother and sister elders that volunteerism is one of the few areas in which we can express ourselves. It validates our position as able and active contributors to society.

Volunteerism offers a generous smorgasbord of useful, interesting and, in many cases, exciting projects. Many of us realize that for the first time in our lives *we select* the job we want to do. We choose the role we want to play. We choose the areas of service to which we want to contribute. Our minds, our abilities, our expertise, our life experience become important and valuable.

So do our hearts. Volunteerism provides an opportunity to be kind to and thoughtful of others. It is exhilarating. In our years of scrabbling to make a living there weren't many such opportunities. The godliness within us that has been atrophied for so long is reborn and refreshed.

As volunteers, we serve the sick and the lonely. We work with children and help the handicapped. We become angels of mercy planning, visiting and helping the lonely. The lost, the abandoned, the wretched, the miserable take courage as the result of our caring. So much of what volunteers do is God's work.

In his poem *Ulysses,* Alfred Lord Tennyson (1809–92) wrote:

> How dull it is to pause,
>   to make an end,
> To rust unburnished,
>   not to shine in use!
> As though to breathe
>   were life.

Further in the same poem, he wrote:

> Death closes all: but
>   something ere the end,
> Some work of noble note,
>   may yet be done,
> Not unbecoming (to) men
>   that strove with gods.

We get down to earth. Poetry, after all, reveals only the tone of volunteerism. We take a quick look at some of the "requests for volunteers" sent back in just two county RSVP (Retired Senior Volunteer Program) departments.

For college-trained people, the Educational Assistance Center of the Criminal Justice Unit has a women offenders project. It wants women for outside visitations and for potential social services for offenders. It offers "on the job" training for this activity.

Center for Energy Policy and Research, N.Y. Institute of Technology. No special requirements for hot-line volunteers. Operators handle telephone inquiries using prepared question and answer cards.

County Work-Release Facility. "We need volunteers: (1) someone who can conduct a guitar music workshop group; (2) someone to teach pottery and ceramics; (3) someone who might want to supervise recreational services from 5 to 10 P.M."

From a mental health center: "Volunteers wanted to assist vocational instructor. Others to be Mental Health Therapy Aides. Also assistants are needed by our Food Services Director."

Some comment is needed on the next volunteer project. In Hempstead, New York, elementary school students had been, for years, *automatically* promoted from grade to grade. Their ability to master the advanced work of the higher grade had nothing to do with their being pushed ahead or promoted.

As expected, the result of this policy was that these students were sent on to high school unprepared for advanced study. Some students could neither read nor write. Nor could they do simple arithmetic. Educationally, the students took a beating. The three R's took a beating too.

The Superintendent of Schools in Hempstead put a stop to this automatic promotion policy. Teachers were instructed not to pass students who failed to meet the accepted standards of the grades they taught. The number of retentions was horrendous. A large percentage of the elementary school population was left back.

A call went out for volunteers to help upgrade the Hempstead educational system. Adelphi University Outreach Project undertook to provide volunteers. The call was *both* for senior volunteers and for high school students. The volunteers conducted one-hour tutoring sessions twice weekly.

It's good to report that the change in the Hempstead promotion system proved acceptable both to parents and students. As of this writing when students at Hempstead schools move ahead they're *ready* for their advanced classes.

We could go on describing the wide variety of services performed by volunteers. We could list the titles of the programs, their content, the specific areas of their work. But this would make a fat book, five thousand pages long. You have more than 3 million people helping others. You're bound to get thousands of different kinds of volunteer assistance.

Nor could a single volume of manageable size include a list of all the different types of national and local *sponsors* of volunteer services. The organizations and corporations involved in this work would also require a book.

Let's agree, therefore, that volunteerism is big stuff and take it from there. Let's accept the fact that within the limits of their abilities, individual volunteers are trained for the work they elect to do. What's the next step? Should not the *directors* of volunteer programs also be trained for their *managerial* activities?

The beginnings of such managerial training for volunteers are now evident. At Adelphi University on Long Island a Center on Volunteerism has been funded by the W. K. Kellogg Foundation. The money involved is $153,189. The training program is expected to draw *planners* and executives of private and government agencies who head the "volunteer community."

The Center on Volunteerism is designed as a three-year educational, informational and action study program. It will reach out to all who recruit and train volunteers. It is the first demonstration project of its kind in the country. Agency officers, prominent individual volunteers, representatives of government, educational and corporate directors of local Long Island volunteer services will attend.

Such a program is badly needed. The Adelphi program is a first. It should be watched closely by the social studies departments of colleges and universities over the country. It is a step forward in the effective organization and use of volunteers. It will make volunteerism itself more productive. It will make it more rewarding to the volunteers themselves. It will assure interaction among the many volunteer programs where cooperative activities are likely to be helpful.

Should not activist organizations of elders push for similar programs in their local educational institutions?

The umbrella federal agency for volunteer services is called ACTION. Basically, ACTION is oriented toward anti-poverty services in general. Examples would be the Foster Grandparents Program and VISTA.

But the growth of projects like the Retired Senior Volunteer Program (RSVP) presents a problem. RSVP recruits elders who serve both the aging who are poor and those who are comfortably fixed.

Many elders who are involved in the management of RSVP and other such non-poverty volunteer projects now believe that their programs should be taken over by the Administration on Aging (AoA) in the Department of Health, Education and Welfare.

This, in the opinion of many, would be a logical change. It would recognize and confirm the fact that elders, poor, middle-income or even rich, require assistance which has nothing whatever to do with their income or lack of income.

The struggle to separate volunteer services for the elderly from a poverty-minded program like ACTION is important. A special federal project under the aegis of the Administration on Aging would be separately financed and directed. It would recognize the differences between our problems as elders and those where money alone can help.

We elders are concerned with such matters as loneliness. We need protection from criminals. We have health problems. We have educational interests. Those of us who want to re-enter the mainstream of life should be encouraged and re-educated to take on new and significant roles in American society.

A special project of this kind under AoA would appeal to elder volunteers interested in improving the quality of life for their contemporaries. It would also help us to train the kind of younger people who could help our volunteers carry on our work. Thus, it would also improve the style of work by volunteers young and old, and enrich the content of their generous-hearted activities.

We elders should fight for the changeover of volunteer services by our age groups to the Administration on Aging. Meanwhile, of course, we should be supporting the work of ACTION where volunteerism begins. We'll need to start with ACTION and move on from there.

Here, therefore, are the ten regional addresses of AC-
TION offices and the areas of the country these offices cover:

ACTION REGIONAL OFFICES

ACTION Region I
John W. McCormack Federal Bldg.
Room 1420
Boston, Massachusetts 02109
(Vermont, New Hampshire, Maine, Massachusetts, Rhode
Island, Connecticut)
(617) 223-4501

ACTION Region II
26 Federal Plaza
Room 1611
New York, New York 10007
(New York, New Jersey, Puerto Rico, the Virgin Islands)
(212) 264-5710

ACTION Region III
320 Walnut Street, 6th Floor
Philadelphia, Pennsylvania 19106
(Pennsylvania, Delaware, Maryland, West Virginia, Virginia, District of Columbia)
(215) 597-9972

ACTION Region IV
730 Peachtree Street, N.E.
Room 895
Atlanta, Georgia 30308
(Kentucky, Tennessee, North Carolina, South Carolina, Ala-
bama, Mississippi, Georgia, Florida)
(404) 257-3337

ACTION Region V
1 North Wacker Drive
Room 322
Chicago, Illinois 60606
(Minnesota, Wisconsin, Michigan, Illinois, Indiana, Ohio)
(312) 353-5107

ACTION Region VI
212 North St. Paul Street
Room 1600
Dallas, Texas 75201
(New Mexico, Oklahoma, Texas, Arkansas, Louisiana)
(214) 749-1361

ACTION Region VII
2 Gateway Center
4th and State Streets
Room 330
Kansas City, Kansas 66101
(Nebraska, Iowa, Kansas, Missouri)
(816) 758-4486

ACTION Region VIII
1845 Sherman Street
Denver, Colorado 80203
(Montana, North Dakota, South Dakota, Utah, Colorado, Wyoming)
(303) 327-2671

ACTION Region IX
211 Main Street
Fifth Floor

San Francisco, California 94105
(California, Nevada, Arizona, Hawaii, Guam, American Samoa)
(415) 556-1736

ACTION Region X
1601 Second Avenue
Seattle, Washington 98101
(Washington, Oregon, Idaho, Alaska)
(206) 399-4520

What are we waiting for? Let's get to work on this activity. Everybody benefits!

19

Elders: Senior Centers

If you're sixty years old or older, you'll remember. During our childhood one or both of our grandparents lived with us. Some of us actually shared a bedroom with a grandparent. We were the "little ones" in what the sociologists of today call the "extended family"—three generations under one roof.

Nostalgia gentles our memories of those times. We are inclined to think warmly of the past. We don't remember such things as quarrels. The constant bickering between our grandparents and Pop or Mom seemed natural. We kids were often the causes of that bickering. In those days, as now, grandparents' ideas of child raising differed sharply from Pop's and Mom's ideas.

Only in farm households did our grandparents rule the roost. Logically enough. Grandparents *owned* the land. They were the bosses. That's why so many children, now grown-ups, left the farms as soon as they could.

Of course, we children weren't the only causes of dissension. Grandparents on Papa's side complained about the way Mom treated Pop. On Mom's side, complaints stemmed from actions by our father toward Mom's parents. In either case, the situation was often less than peaceful.

Stated simply, in the extended family, most grandparents were something of a nuisance. At best, they were tolerated. At worst, they were disliked. In some families they were hated by one parent or the other.

In those days, religious institutions and social organizations began to provide some relief for our mothers and fathers. They opened their vestry rooms or social halls to the elderly. Generally, these became known as "golden age clubs." Our grandmothers joined these clubs. Except for the card players, our grandfathers stayed scornfully away from club activities.

This was the beginning of what came to be known later as senior clubs. Meetings were held once or several afternoons a week. Our fathers and mothers heaved sighs of relief. Grandma now had a place to spend a few hours away from the house.

We who are now elders were then in our twenties or younger. We, therefore, didn't see it. But at that time qualitative changes were taking place in the attitude of the nation toward the aged. We moved out of our parents' homes. Our grandparents died off. Nowadays a vast majority of us who are elders live away from our grown children. We go to visit their homes when we're invited to baby-sit our grandchildren. The nuclear family came into being.

Translate the term "nuclear family." You come up with "no room in the house for us elders."

This change triggered a vast amount of theoretical writing about the "plight of the aged." It led to the development of some practical social services for the over-sixty population. We elders were recognized as a separate group with special problems.

By the end of World War II courses in gerontology were being listed in many colleges and universities. By the 1975–76 year, the National Directory of Educational Programs in Gerontology could list 1,275 colleges and universities offering "programs" and/or degrees in gerontology.

Many positive benefits are now being provided as a result of all this concern for, and interest in us elders. We can see improvements in some of the availabilities to the aged of which this book has been somewhat critical. Yes, we'll need to push hard for more improvements. But if we do push, we'll get results.

The most positive developments took place among the senior clubs. They stopped being just places where old women sat around swapping pictures of grandchildren. They stopped being gossip gatherings. The directors of these clubs began to set up programs which reached out and challenged our individual and our collective talents.

Trips were arranged for us. People with expertise in varied handicrafts taught their specialties. Members who were good at woodworking or sewing, painting or quilting, helped brother and sister elders to master different productive skills. There was less time for chitchat, more time for creativity. The sense of "belonging" to a senior club changed to active participation in a wider selection of programs.

The next forward step was the setting up of senior centers. These were full-time, full-service institutions. They were open from 10 A.M. to 4 P.M. five days a week. They offered an even wider choice of activities than did the senior clubs.

The directors and staff of these centers were usually trained social workers with specialized experience in work with the aging. Programs were not laid on. The membership committees elected by members represented the views, aspirations and interests of the membership. They worked *with* the directors.

Over the past ten years, the centers have expanded. The number, variety and content of programs grew. Senior clubs had, as a rule, emphasized mainly social and recreational activities. Centers became community agents. They coordinated priority services for the aged as described in the Older Americans Act.

A well-run senior center covers a wide choice of activities beyond recreation. There are physical fitness programs. There are planned trips to museums. There are lectures on health and cultural subjects. Choral groups are organized and led in their singing by professional directors brought into the centers for this purpose.

It took about ten years for the values of the senior centers to be recognized by their local Area Agencies on Aging (AAAs). Until recently, the Area Agencies on Aging failed to understand the multi-faceted character of such centers. This, in spite of the fact that almost one third of the Title III projects of the Older Americans Act were aimed at the extension of senior center activities.

An article by Eugene Paul Bartell, Director of Baltimore (Md.) City Area on Aging appeared in the March-April 1978 issue of *Perspective on Aging*, published by the National Council on the Aging.

Bartell heads his article, "What is the AAA Link?"

"In Baltimore, we have been both challenged and excited by the senior center *concept*. We see centers as the vehicle by which the area agency can give substance to the Older Americans Act at community and neighborhood levels.

"The service delivery system for the elderly across the country may be seen as a kaleidoscope of shifting patterns. There appears to be little coordination among health care, income-benefit programs, in-home services and social support services. Services that provide similar functions and which ideally should be grouped together are frequently separated in practice.

"Area Agency directors, heads of senior centers and the elderly are all victims of this fragmented process. It impedes the progress of coordinating related services for older persons. As a result, the service provided deals with only one aspect of the person's life when, actually, clients' needs are manifold and cut across service lines. Reducing such fragmentation is clearly a goal senior centers can serve by bringing together under one roof the diversity of services and community resources for the elderly."

Now let's go back a bit. We've traced briefly the history of the ingathering of local groups of the aging through four stages—from small local senior groups, to golden age clubs, to senior citizen clubs, to the birth of senior centers. It's a good progression, a healthy progression.

Now we come to multi-purpose senior centers. These set specific goals to which the Area Agencies on Aging can address their efforts.

Mr. Bartell explores these possibilities in the following manner:

"A range of services from different agencies can be grouped together in a multi-purpose senior center. These would facilitate cooperative approaches among social agencies dealing with the elderly. They would enhance accessibility. They would diminish transportation difficulties and eliminate all barriers to handicapped elders. They would reduce confusion and bewilderment over bureaucratic procedures. In a multi-purpose facility, the needs of the whole person can be positively responded to in a manner not possible for a single service agency. The elderly can be directly involved in program planning and efforts that promote self-determination.

"The multi-purpose senior center has broad appeal to older persons from diversified socio-economic backgrounds. There has proven to be a high rate of acceptance and use by the elderly when multi-purpose centers are available."

The National Council on the Aging (NCOA) reports that five thousand senior centers now are in operation throughout the nation. But the NCOA uses the word "centers" loosely. How many of these "centers" are just local senior clubs? How many, or rather how few, *deserve* to be called multi-purpose centers?

The job ahead for present and soon-to-be elders is clear enough. Wherever we live and however we live, there should be a multi-purpose senior center in operation.

This is not basically a question of money. That has largely been answered by Title V of the Older Americans Act (OAA). More than $300 million is being spent yearly for operation, expansion and construction of multi-purpose senior centers. In the 1977 fiscal year $40 million was spent under Title V of the Older Americans Act for building, altering or renovating facilities to serve as multi-purpose senior centers for us elders.

Title III of the OAA also has money for comprehensive services which multi-purpose centers should be providing. These often include transportation, outreach, home chore services, information and referral.

And Title IV of the OAA is another source of funds. It is for the training and upgrading the work of staffs at centers so that they can assist elders more effectively.

The multi-purpose center in any community should control the delivery of services to the elders of that community on a twenty-four-hour-a-day basis. At its best it establishes a network of satellites or branches operating at neighborhood levels. The most efficient centers link up with senior club programs to assure that elders have access to all activities and services.

Title V explains the distinguishing characteristics of multi-purpose centers in terms of four main areas. These are group services and activities; individual services; geographical accessibility without barriers to the handicapped; interrelationships with public and private social agencies.

Group services in this view should include

1. Recreation for physical health and socialization.
2. A variety of educational opportunities.
3. Programs for sharing information.
4. Mutual concern sessions which expand support mechanisms.
5. Congregate meals and social events.

Hold on to that "congregate meals" bit for a few paragraphs. We'll sum up the value of multi-purpose centers first.

To be worthy of the name, each multi-purpose center should have an organized plan for delivery of all needed advisory services. These would include individual and collective guidance. They would help solve:

1. Health, legal, financial and housing matters.
2. Neighborhood problems such as protection against criminal attack.
3. Protection against gyp artists who prey on the aging.
4. Personal problems such as arguments with retailers, landlords, young neighbors.

In providing such advisory services, the multi-purpose center should offer the services of volunteer or professional personnel. These would represent elders before city, county and state political officials when necessary.

We need to assume, of course, that cultural, social and recreational activities will go right along with these advisory and assistance services.

The number of elders we are talking about and their description were outlined in *Aging* magazine, May-June 1978. *Aging* is the official publication of the Administration on Aging. *Aging* summarizes the situation of clubs and centers as follows:

"More than five million older Americans, from 60 to 95 years of age (about one-quarter are 75 or older), are members and participants in the country's more than 5,000 senior centers, according to the National Institute of Senior Centers.

"More than half of the participants live alone compared with one-third of the general elderly population who live alone.

"They come from all economic backgrounds. Among those who attended these centers, 47 percent were blue collar workers, 16 percent, white collar workers, and 16 percent, professionals, according to the Institute.

"In any given two-week period, about six percent of all older Americans attend a senior center, according to data collected for the Institute by Louis Harris & Associates. About 18 percent have attended a senior center 'recently.' Another 18 percent would like to attend a center. The most frequent reason they do not is that no facility is available."

With these statistics in mind, we can discuss further the "congregate meals" situation. We can take it for granted that elders who go to multi-purpose centers eat a hot lunch there. What about the many elders who can't get to a multi-purpose center? What about those who live where there is no multi-purpose center to which they can go? Where do they eat? What do they eat? How do they eat?

For such elders, a generous government has set up Title VII of the Older Americans Act. Stripped of its legal verbiage, Title VII aims to provide *"one nourishing hot meal daily for every older American."* It's called the Nutrition Program.

By any standards, the Nutrition Program is one of the truly great services we elders have going for us. It is special in many ways. Particularly, it is the *only* service for the aging in the United States which does not require a "means" test. It is not necessary to prove poverty in order to participate. Nutrition centers should be developed as multi-purpose centers.

Rich, middle-income and poor elders can come to, or be brought to, a nutrition center to eat a good meal in the company of contemporaries. Elders may drive to a nutrition center in a Cadillac. They can be brought by bus. They can walk. If they can reach the center, they can eat. If they are shut-ins and can't get to the center, their meals will be brought to them.

Some nutrition centers do charge a small fee for the meals. But most leave it up to the elders themselves to make a donation. The money wealthier elders contribute covers the expenses for those who can't pay.

In some parts of the country, congregate meals are delivered by catering services at so much per meal. That's paid for by the local office of aging. But most meals are prepared on the premises. Menus are often policed under the supervision of *elected* councils of elder users.

We have in the nutrition centers a very encouraging and valuable phenomenon. Many of us object strongly to the term "senior citizen." Anyone who gets to be sixty years old or older automatically becomes a senior citizen. The term is strictly based on age. It tells nothing about the person. The nutrition centers have made it possible to separate those who are "elders" from those who are merely senior citizens. Multi-purpose centers and nutrition centers as a *combination* of services attract both types of elderly persons.

We go back in history. We discover that the *elders* of any community were the leaders, the guides, the activists in that community. They were admired for their wisdom, their sagacity, their involvement in community life. In spite of their age? No. *Because* of their age.

In present-day society age groups are differentiated as much by what they can contribute as they are by age. Such differentiation puts older Americans into the same grouping as children and those in early youth. Calling us senior citizens assumes that older people are receivers of services rather than *contributors*.

We will grant that those of us who spend retirement years

playing games and watching television deserve to be called senior citizens. They are able people. Yet they make no contribution to their own age group. They do nothing for society as a whole.

Elders among us are those who continue to *contribute* as activists both to our own age group and to society. We cite the performance of 3.5 million volunteers who participate in the lives of others. Anyone who helps others, young or old, in *any* way automatically deserves the honor of being called an "elder."

Recently a new publication called *Elderworks* appeared. The first issue answered the question, "Who are the elders?" Here is the answer to that question.

"They're Americans of every stripe, type and condition who want new opportunities to use their skills and experiences in ways that will benefit others. They are impatient to embark upon new involvements. They seek intellectual challenges provided by serving others. They look for volunteer positions in education, health care, and legal and other services."

Reader, are you a senior citizen or an elder?

20

Elders as Crime Victims

It took considerable digging. We wanted to get reliable raw figures on crimes against the aged. We searched in the press. We consulted the political pooh-bahs. We went to the academicians and to the national senior citizens organizations. We studied research reports in the areas of gerontology, criminology, urban planning and the behavioral sciences.

We finally uncovered an exhaustive report published by the Sub-Committee on Housing and Consumer Interests of the congressional Select Committee on Aging. It is entitled *In Search of Security*. The subtitle is "A National Perspective on Elderly Crime Victimization."

Chairman is Edward R. Roybal (D. Cal.). Ranking Minority Member of the Committee on Aging is John Paul Hammerschmidt (R. Ark.).

To begin with, the committee report admitted that surveys and studies (on the subject of crime against elders) have been diverse and contradictory. That puts it mildly.

The Federal Bureau of Investigation (FBI), for example, gets information on crime from 9,160 state and local law enforcement agencies. An odd fact emerges. The FBI knows who the *criminals* are. The data they receive state the age, sex and race of the *criminal* perpetrators. *They do not record the age of the victims!*

Asked by Chairman Roybal about this strange failure to identify *victims* of crime by age, the FBI director said, "Age data on victims is not required in what we call our uniform crime reporting system. That reporting system asks for age, sex and race information about the person *arrested*. To add statistics about the victim would be quite an extension and quite expensive."

Roybal: I don't understand how it would be expensive.

Kelly: Just the time consumed in developing all this information.

Roybal: But in a report that is made, could not a police department ask the age of the victim?

The colloquy went on in that vein. Kelly concluded his testimony. "Yes, recording the age of victims is a method of compiling some useful data. Nonetheless, it is expensive and it does cause some problems."

Far be it from us elders to put the FBI to extra expense! And certainly the FBI has enough problems. We also know how tight the FBI budget has been. They may well be on the road to poverty. But adding a "blip" to their computers which would tell the age of victims of crime is unlikely to cost too much.

Our search for specific data on crimes against the elderly continued. We checked the Law Enforcement Assistance Administration (LEAA). This administration was added to the Department of Justice. It was created to assist and supplement *local* law enforcement agencies.

One of its functions is to conduct studies and gather data on incidence of crime.

The National Crime Panel of the LEAA has undertaken five surveys on criminal victimization in the United States. These reports constitute the most extensive attempt to document the risk of being victimized that different groups in our society encounter. The crimes which are measured are those considered most serious by the general public and which lend themselves to measurement by the survey method. For individuals, these are: rape, robbery, assault and personal larceny; for households: burglary, larceny and motor vehicle theft.

The victimization rates derived from the national study reveal that the elderly are victims of violent crimes at a rate of 8 per 1,000 population. This compares with a rate for the general population at 32 per 1,000 population. For crimes of theft, the elderly are victimized at a rate of 22 per 1,000. This compares to 91 per 1,000 for the general population.

In household crimes, the elderly experience victimization rates of 107 per 1,000 households. The general population has a rate of 217 per 1,000 households. Therefore, according to the survey data, national victimization rates are *lower* for the elderly than for the general population.

Theoretically, then, according to these LEAA figures and according to the data provided by other LEAA surveys, we elders should stop screaming. We are not disproportionately victimized.

The sub-committee believes, however, that the general figures mask certain crime categories in which the elderly experience high victimization rates. According to *Criminal*

Victimization Surveys in the Nation's Five Largest Cities, the elderly have the *highest* rates of larceny with contact in four out of the five cities.

In *Crime in Eight American Cities,* it is revealed that while the victimization rate for the general population for personal larceny with contact is 317 per 100,000, the rate for those fifty to sixty-four is 342 per 100,000, and 362 per 100,000 for those sixty-five and older. In three of the eight cities, robbery with injury was highest for those fifty and over.

Although the elderly appear to be less victimized in most of the crime categories of the LEAA survey than persons in younger age groups, this is just one way of viewing the data.

Another way to utilize the data is to examine the raw figures. In the sub-committee hearing held on April 12, 1976, in Washington, D.C., Henry F. McQuade, Deputy Administrator for Policy Development of the Law Enforcement Assistance Administration, provided the following figures:

1. In crimes of violence, the elderly experience 8 victimizations per 1,000 population.

2. In crimes of theft, 22 victimizations per 1,000 population.

3. In household crimes, 107 victimizations per 1,000 population.

If the elderly population at that time was approximately 20 million, in a one-year period the elderly experienced 160,000 violent crimes, 440,000 crimes of theft and 2,140,000 household crimes. Combining these figures, we find that the elderly experience 2,740,000 crimes per 20 million population. This means that an elderly person stands a *little better than one chance in ten of being the victim of a crime in a one-year period.*

Another valuable use of these data is a comparison of the victimization rates of the elderly for consecutive years to determine any changes over time. The report *Criminal Victimization in the United States: A Comparison of 1973 and 1974* states that Americans sixty-five years of age and older experienced *the greatest overall increase in crimes of violence.* There was a 46 per cent increase in assault during that one-year period. Although robbery for males without injury decreased 28.4 per cent, robbery *with* injury for males increased 25.4 per cent. Personal larceny with contact increased 14.4 per cent. Personal larceny without contact increased 11.2 per cent for females.

In the aggregate figure for crimes of violence for both sexes, there was a 6.5 per cent increase between 1973 and 1974 (males 10.9, females 1.8). The aggregate figure for crimes of theft shows a decrease of 1.9 per cent. This figure is deceiving since a breakdown by sex shows that although males have experienced a decrease of 14.3 per cent, theft against females *increased* by 11.7 per cent. In fact, the increase in theft for females sixty-five and older is higher than for any age group in the survey.

From our standpoint as elders the quantitative figures are less important than the qualitative effects of crimes against us. We are vulnerable physically. We are damaged financially. We are hurt psychologically. Any crime against an older person has elements of all three of these factors. When criminally attacked, no group of victims of crime in our country *suffers* more than we do.

It becomes a question of impact. The theft of a television set devastates us. Somehow, younger people will replace the stolen set. They can buy a new set on time payments. Most elders, however, are considered high credit risks and cannot get time payment acceptance.

The rip-off of a handbag with a month's Social Security money in it is a question of food and rent. Medicare, moreover, doesn't pay for prescription drugs, which all but a few lucky elders among us need.

At this writing, there is only one national program to help elders learn how to avoid victimization. The American Association of Retired Persons (AARP), which is allied with the National Retired Teachers Association (NRTA), has developed a comprehensive manual and training program emphasizing the "prevention of crime through personal action."

Originally, the educational program of AARP/NRTA was limited to local chapters. It is now being made available to nutrition centers, civic, church and private organizations. The goals of the program aim (1) to minimize criminal victimization among elders, (2) to reduce criminal opportunity and (3) to reduce unwarranted or exaggerated fear.

The training program for elders offers four two-hour workshops. These cover:

1. Street crime: The most frequent crimes and how to avoid them.
2. Burglary: How to protect the home.
3. Fraud: Confidence schemes, white-collar crime.
4. Community and police relations: How we elders should work with police to reduce crime.

In line with this, AARP/NRTA has also developed a workshop for police and other law enforcement officials. The aim there is to increase their sensitivity to crime-related problems of elders.

In this instance, certain positive acts are called for. Activists among us have an enormous stake in spreading this anticrime education in our own communities. AARP/NRTA locals nationwide must first check whether the police in *their* areas have taken the police sensitivity course. They must develop plans to carry the education plan for elder safety *beyond* the AARP/NRTA locals.

It will be necessary to spread the word. Committees from the AARP/NRTA locals should fan out first to other activist groups and organizations of elders in their areas. They and other interested activists should seek out elders who, because of the neighborhoods in which they live, are most at risk to predators. For further information about the AARP/NRTA program, write George Sunderland, Senior Coordinator, AARP/NRTA, 1909 K Street, N.W., Washington, D.C. 20049.

We elders, it seems, are not really safe anywhere. We must, therefore, protect each other. We must devise programs and undertake activities on the basis of one for all, and all for one.

Members of AARP/NRTA, for example, are generally middle-income or well-to-do retirees. They live in the better environments in cities or suburbs. Yet, because they are old, their physical stamina is diminished. They suffer hearing and visual losses. They incur ailments such as arthritis and circulatory diseases. The bones of middle-income elders are as easily broken as the bones of less affluent elders.

But the neighborhoods in which they live are changing. For years they were safe. Now they are becoming high-crime-rate areas. Often they can't move to new communities.

More than 60 per cent of the elderly have lived for decades in central cities or in areas contiguous to central cities. Statistically, elders are more likely to live alone. A criminal is more apt to burglarize a house inhabited by one elderly person. An elder is a target for criminals on the streets or on public transportation. The more comfortable elders who are socially isolated are particularly susceptible to fraud, bunco and confidence games.

We cite the data on criminals from four cities where statistics were kept on the offenders. The Wilmington, Delaware, Crime Resistance Task Force reports as follows:

> Age: 13 to 21 years of age in 85 per cent of 174 arrest-related samples.
> Sex and Race: Black male 92 per cent of 203 perpetrators.
> Environment: The offender often lives within ten blocks of the victim.

Detroit, Michigan: The Detroit Cass Corridor Study.

> Age: 66 per cent in age group 13 to 18. The remaining were in the 19 to 25 age group.
> Race: 82 per cent were black. Approximately 98 per cent were male.

A Houston Model Neighborhood Area Study

> Age: 92 per cent were under 45.
> Race (not rates but cases): 51 were black, 24 were white, 15 were Mexican-Americans. Over 93 per cent were male.

A Kansas City report states that "The most salient fact in this study is that the young Americans are attacking, stealing and generally victimizing the *old*." Here are the figures which prove that statement in Kansas City:

59.7 per cent were teenagers.

29.5 per cent were in their twenties.

6.7 per cent were in their thirties.

2.8 per cent were middle-aged.

1.3 per cent were older persons.

Race (suspects): 84.2 per cent were black. 15.2 per cent were white.

Sex: 94.3 per cent were male. 5.7 per cent were female.

The consolidation of all available data shows that 59.7 per cent of the offenders were teenagers and 29.5 per cent were in their twenties. Therefore, nearly 90 per cent of the offenders were under thirty years of age.

For almost every crime category, the majority of offenders were black (84.2 per cent). (Historically, police departments have often patrolled minority areas more heavily, resulting in higher arrest records for blacks.)

White offenders, however, constituted 59.5 per cent of all *fraud* cases. The majority of offenders in all categories of crime, other than fraud, were males.

There are also some interesting correlations between the age of the offender and the type of crime committed. For example, burglaries are the most frequent crimes committed by teenagers. Offenders in their twenties and thirties most often commit armed robbery.

Statistics gathered in this study also support the theory that crime is more frequently intraracial rather than interracial. This reflects the housing patterns of the area. Offenders, especially the young, generally commit crimes in or near their own neighborhoods. Therefore, older white people who live in predominantly white areas are victimized by whites. Blacks who live in predominantly black areas are victimized by blacks.

The elderly white people who live in the inner city are generally clustered together in larger *integrated* areas. They are, therefore, subject to being victimized by offenders of both races.

The statistics which break down the age, race and sex of criminals in these four cities do not vary sharply in other cities and their nearby surburbs.

Bureau of Labor statistics for 1973 show that almost half of elders sixty-five and over are retired. We live on fixed incomes. Our "poverty" level at the time was $2,505 for a couple, $1,974 for an individual. In older families, 12 per cent were below poverty level. For the person living alone, 37 per cent were living below the poverty level.

In 1973, also, the Bureau of Labor statistics indicated that costs to maintain an "intermediate" retired couple were a minimum of $5,414 yearly. Half of us could not maintain that adequate standard of living then. Now in 1979 our conditions are appreciably worse as a result of inflation.

Hence, it is obvious that the theft of $20 from an elder presents a greater *relative* loss than the same amount stolen from an employed person. We have no bank accounts. We live month to month on our Social Security, our pensions, our Supplemental Security Income checks.

What price fear? All data available indicate that we elders are being forced to live out our days and nights in fear of crime. The fear of crime in rural areas is 19 per cent. In large cities fear of crime rises to 71 per cent. But all of us share the fear of crime to some degree. The behavioral changes among us elderly were recorded as follows:

1. Eighty-four per cent would not walk after dark, with 62 per cent attributing this directly to the fear of crime.

2. Almost 25 per cent of all those interviewed avoided certain areas in their own neighborhoods due to fear.

3. Sixty-six and two thirds per cent felt their homes would be burglarized.

4. Fifty-four per cent avoided certain areas of the city because they felt them to be unsafe, and their perception of the city as a whole was fraught with anxiety.

It's good to report on one result of this particular research. In Multnomah County, Oregon, the homes of elder residents have been made safer against burglary. Locks have been put in doors. Windows which might permit intruders to enter have been repaired. An educational program has been set up.

It is good to report also that practical programs like those in the Portland, Oregon, area are proliferating. Yes, they vary in content. There are silly ideas like supplying whistles to elders under attack. There are sensible ideas like involving high-schoolers in escort services when we go shopping. Drivers of cars or mini-bus service take us where we want to go.

There's no lack of willing help for us elders in many communities. What's missing, however, is an organized, consistent federal plan aimed at securing the safety of American elders everywhere.

This could be a variant of H.R. 3686, which was nixed in the House of Representatives in the 95th Congress. H.R. 3686 was called the Victims of Crime Act of 1977. Its purpose was to compensate victims of criminal actions against citizens for losses due to crime.

H.R. 3686 would have provided block grants to states now already compensating victims of crime. It would also provide an incentive to states that do *not* yet have a program which compensates victims of crimes. The thinking was "Since crime is a *national* social issue, federally financed support money for compensation should be made available in all states."

We can understand why the Congress didn't pass H.R. 3686. It took in altogether too much territory. It would have cost the feds many millions of dollars.

But if a bill were introduced in Congress which recognized the special, the unique problems of *elderly* victims of crimes, wouldn't it cost much less? Such a bill would establish the following rules:

1. That victims sixty-two years of age or older, with annual taxable incomes as defined by Section 61 of the Internal Revenue Code, would be compensated for property loss. There should be no minimum for compensation. However, a maximum of $1,000 would be established. (In order to minimize administrative costs, a simplified process is recommended for losses under $100.)

2. Medical expenses for a victim sixty-two or older not covered by Medicare or Medicaid would be compensated.

3. Emergency assistance for such items as food, medicine, rent, utilities and other essentials would be provided for the elderly crime victim. The cost of this

assistance would be recovered from any compensation that the victim would receive.

4. Police agencies would be required to furnish application forms and provide assistance to the victim in completing the forms. This could easily be accomplished by the establishment of a "victim advocate" by police departments.

5. The existence of the elderly victim compensation program would be widely publicized. Hospitals licensed under state or federal laws or using federal assistance would be required to display posters in their emergency rooms. These would contain detailed information on the existence and provisions of the program. Posters emphasizing the special provision for assistance to the elderly would also be displayed at Social Security offices, senior centers, nutrition sites and senior citizen housing projects.

We elders see such a program as a first step in reducing the effects of crime against us. The states and communities would be required to add their own money to the federal investment. There would be a qualitative change in the approach to solving the problem of crime against the elderly. States, cities and communities would be forced to beef up protection of elders in order to save money.

The introduction in Congress of a bill of this kind might force states, counties and communities to rethink their plans to protect us elders.

Will *your* congressional representative introduce such a bill? That's up to you, dear reader. Write to your congressman if you agree with me.

21

Elders: The Minorities

Fancy talk about equality in the United States is 83 per cent hogwash. Equality has a label which in the South and West is "For whites only." In the North, it reads "For whites mostly."

In this country the *color* of people's skin usually determines whether or not they get out of the ghettos. The Irish came. They lived for a while in ghettos. They managed to pull themselves out of the ghettos; and so did the Jews, the immigrants from Europe. The whites made it. Non-white minorities did not. Blacks, Mexican-Americans, Puerto Ricans and Indians account for one sixth to one seventh of our population. In a report entitled *Minorities in the United States* by Levitan, Johnston and Taggart ($3.50, Public Affairs Press, 419 New Jersey Ave., S.E., Washington, D.C. 20003) we get statistics as follows:

In 1973, there were 32.5 million colored minorities.

Quoting the report:

"The 1970 census statistics, though questionable on some counts, leave no doubt about these gaps in income, employment and education. The mean per capita income of Blacks, Mexican-Americans, Puerto Ricans, and Indians in 1969 was less than 54 percent that of all whites. Minorities accounted for more than a third of the poor and nearly two-fifths of all families receiving welfare. Comparatively, Blacks had slightly greater per capita income. Together both of the Spanish minorities had fewer persons in poverty. Indians were worst off on all counts.

"Employment problems are the major cause of low income. Black, Mexican-American, Puerto Rican, and Indian workers are concentrated in low-paying, unstable jobs at the bottom of the occupational ladder. In 1970, they were twice as likely as whites to be in service or laboring occupations.

"Their unemployment rate was almost three-fourths higher than for whites. They accounted for a fifth of the unemployed, though, they were only an eighth of the labor force. Minority males experience lower labor force participation rates and more frequent work interruptions than whites.

"Except for Indians, whose status in depressed reservation economies is far worse than that of any other group, Blacks suffer the greatest occupational and employment handicaps, with more workers in service and laboring jobs and with higher rates of male unemployment and non-participation in the labor force."

Our concern here, of course, is for the elderly among these minorities. We can say for certain that if the statistics cover the data about these minorities of all ages, the *aged* among them are triply discriminated against.

All minorities, young and old, have suffered, and still

suffer deprivations of various kinds primarily because of their color. Generalized comparisons among the blacks, Puerto Ricans, Mexican-Americans and Indians are difficult to make. Indians, for example, are literally a conquered nation and live that way on their reservations.

Puerto Ricans, who are concentrated mainly on the East Coast, lag substantially behind averages in nearly all dimensions of socio-economic status. Birth rates are high. In New York, Puerto Rican women average 3.2 children per family. That's one third more than white New York families.

Yet, because the faces of all these minorities are colored in shades from black to tan, they experience almost identical difficulties.

It is true that, except for the Indians, all the colored minorities have made substantial gains since 1960. Chicanos, Mexican-Americans and Puerto Ricans have seen their incomes rise and their educational facilities expand. Nevertheless, they are still the low people on the totem pole. And their elderly population is located at the very bottom of that pole.

On March 25, 1977, the congressional Select Committee on Aging, in cooperation with the congressional Black Caucus Brain Trust on Aging, published the following data. We reproduce, with permission of these committees, part of Congressman Claude Pepper's introduction, along with his presentation of the facts.

> Those of us who are aware of the ever-growing sense of alienation and despair that the Black elderly are forced to live with, are also cognizant of the fact that this despair is the result of years of insufficient income, sub-standard housing, inadequate health care, lack of

transportation to needed services, limited educational opportunities, as well as fear of personal harm.

While these are problems that my committee has dealt with and which the majority of our senior citizens face, I am keenly aware of the compounded effect these problems have on Blacks and other minority and low-income aged. We have found, for instance, that:

There are 24.2 million Americans 65 and older or more than 10% of the entire U.S. population of 222 million.

There are 1.8 million Blacks aged 65 and older in the U.S and close to 40% of them lived in poverty in 1975.

Blacks are 12% of the U.S. population, but older Blacks, because of shorter life spans, make up less than 8% of the elderly population. Of aged Blacks living alone, 75% have incomes below the federal poverty line of $2,717, and $3,485 per couple. Of aged black females, over 60% have incomes under $2,000.

We know that in addition to their income being inadequate, the Black elderly live in substandard housing as well. According to government statistics, seven out of ten Black aged Americans live in poverty areas. Also,

Approximately 60% of older Blacks live in the south.

Nearly one out of every five Black homes lacks some or all "desirable plumbing."

One out of every four housing units occupied by non-whites is substandard.

As a result of limited educational opportunities,

many of our Black and other minority and low-income elderly find it impossible to traverse the bureaucratic maze in search of much needed service. Statistics show that:

Over 60% of the Black aged have completed less than seven grades of school.

Of the Black aged, 12% are illiterate compared to 2% of the white elderly.

A lifetime of poverty and neglect has taken its toll on the life expectancy for Blacks. According to a report of the public health service (1974),

The death rates for Blacks exceed those for whites at all ages through 70 years.

The average life expectancy for Black males is 62.9 years compared to 68.9 for whites.

The average life expectancy for Black females is 71.2 years while that for white females is 76.6.

The National Caucus/Center on Black Aged had chosen as their theme, "Health Care and the Black Aged: A Call for Radical Change." For, indeed, it *will* take a radical change in policy to correct the cumulative effects of a lifetime of inadequate medical care, lack of educational opportunities, insufficient income, inferior housing and poor nutrition which have plagued the lives of Blacks and other minority and low-income elderly for far too long.

A comprehensive, coordinated and responsive health care system for *all* the elderly should be our goal. We must strive to insure that when skilled care is needed, it is available for all of our citizens. It is unfortunate that while Blacks comprise 8% of the elderly population, they comprise only 3% of the nursing home population.

[Congressman Pepper concluded] I will be most willing to accept any suggestions for legislative directions that I can take back to the House Select Committee on Aging for further consideration.

As a result of this March 17, 1978, hearing, the Select Committee on Aging of the House of Representatives submitted the following recommendations for changes in the Older Americans Act:

The proposals cover the titles of the OAA as a whole. These are Title III, State and Community Programs; Title V, Multi-purpose Senior Centers; Title IV, Research, Training and Gerontology Centers; Title IX, Employment.

We recommend right here that all activist elders should write to the Select Committee on Aging, 712 Congressional Annex 1, Washington, D.C. 20515, or phone them at (202) 225-9375 for a copy of the March 17, 1978, *Summary of Older Americans Act (OAA) Recommendations*. It provides a blueprint for changes in and expansion of the Older Americans Act.

An example of the first proposals and those which outline *minority* concerns and recommendations is reproduced herewith.

1. *OAA Placement*
   Make the Commissioner on Aging responsible directly to the Secretary of HEW, rather than part of the Office of Human Development Services.

2. *Advocacy*
   (a) The Older Americans Act should specify the advocacy role for area and state agencies, with emphasis on the use of older persons as advocates.
   (b) The nursing home ombudsman program should be given statutory underpinning as part of Title III.

3. The current disregard of nutrition program benefits for purposes of other laws should be broadened to include benefits under *other* titles, including part-time employment at the minimum wage.

4. *Minority concerns*
   (a) Area agencies for the aging should bear responsibility for affirmative action goals.
   (b) U. S. Commission on Civil Rights should study and report on racial discrimination in federally funded aging programs.
   (c) To help compensate for shorter life expectancies of minorities, area agencies should be given authority to waive age 60 for nutrition program participation.
   (d) The National Clearinghouse on Aging should compile and disseminate data on minority elderly.
   (e) An Office of Affirmative Action and Minority Affairs should be created within OAA.
   (f) All parts of Title IV (training, research and gerontology centers) should ensure closer involvement of minority group members.
   (g) Minority issues should be addressed specifically in the 1981 White House Conference on Aging.
   (h) OAA funds distributed to states by formula should take into account the poverty factor which parallels the incidence of minority elderly.
   (i) Indian tribes should receive funds directly from OAA for Older Americans Act programs.

We white elders are a minority of the total population. We cannot afford to sit smugly back and say, "We have our own problems. Let the aged colored minorities fight their own battles as we do."

We grant that white elders have some hope of achieving a measure of success in their struggle for improvements in their lives—not so with the non-white elders.

In this regard, sociologist Mary V. Jennings Wacksman says this in her forthcoming book, *The American Black Elderly:* "We must consider the factors that characterize black lifestyles in black communities. Black communities result from residential segregation. Such segregation forms lifetime patterns. These are characterized as 'kinship networks,' 'living with others'—usually families, but not always so."

We white elders remember well this kind of living from childhood days. It's now called "the extended family." Every able-bodied member worked and added his or her income to the family money pot. Except for the rich, there was no other way for a family to survive.

The big difference for the Blacks and other non-white minorities *within* the extended families was that such jobs as they managed to get paid low wages and were usually temporary. Even in good times, the minorities were the last to be hired and the first to be fired. On the record, "affirmative action" has not corrected this situation for the elderly minorities.

Whites must understand, however, that neglect of the needs of the aging colored minorities inevitably leads to neglect of the white aging as well.

The price of intolerance is high. The price of segregation is higher. The price of hate is highest of all.

We white elders should seek out and welcome our black brother and sister elderly into our own local organizations, as well as the elderly of other minority groups. We should seek out and bring them into our local councils. We should direct special efforts to make them comfortable with us so that we become comfortable with them.

There is need for unity. Struggle is necessary for all elders regardless of color, religion or national origin. Elders must speak with one voice. The white, the black, the tan must work together.

Together, we shall overcome.

22

Elders: Mobile Homes

Most of this book has spared readers the boredom of statistics. But there's no way for me to make my basic points about how mobile homes relate to older Americans without a batch of numbers.

Skim through the data if you like. Skip them entirely if you wish. But first read this letter from the head of a tenant's association in a mobile home park.

"Dear Mr. Cottin, People, like you, who know nothing about mobile homes, decide to purchase one. You have no idea where to go for information or comparison. Dealers and park or court owners do not tell one in advance about set-up, where one can and cannot locate, extras in costs, equipment, labor, etc.

"For example, one must have skirting, tie-downs, utility shed, steps, where required. They say one must purchase these from the court owner or whoever he specifies and pay whatever price they charge.

"No mention is made of entrance or exit fees—as such. If one asks, he's usually told, 'It's not an entrance fee—it's part of the installation or set-up fee.' Yet, one is also told upon purchasing a mobile home that the installation or set-up fee is included in the purchase price.

"Also, one is not forewarned about maybe not being able to get into a court of one's choosing—unless the dealer happens to be 'hand-in-hand' with that particular court owner or manager. Further, buying from some dealers, one may have no choice of parks or even any park available to one.

"Gas rates—some parks have natural gas but some are supplied with propane gas so are not registered with the gas company. So, even tho' we have obtained legislation for reduced rates for retired people on limited incomes, such as regular home owners have, our gas company does not want to allow them this discount."

Interestingly, both the name of the correspondent and that of the state are withheld. The correspondent lives in fear of intimidation and possible "punishment" from the owners of the mobile home park in which he lives. This is a tip-off for what's coming.

Now keep in mind that we are here talking about mobile homes. We are not, in this book, concerned with travel trailers, campers, vans or motor coaches. These can be *moved*. Individuals tow them from place to place on highways.

Under present terminology, what makes a mobile home a mobile home is that it is not *movable*. Once set down in a mobile home park or mobile home court, that's where it stays.

So, the first statistics.

During the years between 1947 and 1971, shipments of mobile homes rose as follows:

1947: 60,000 units; retail value $146,000,000.

1971: 496,570 units; retail value $3,297,225,000.

Here's a comparison between mobile homes and the Site-Built homes as issued by the United States Bureau of Census data (Conventional Homes-Construction Report, February 1972). This is a *sales* comparison based on the *price* of the homes.

MOBILE HOME SHARE OF THE HOUSING MARKET FOR THE YEAR 1971

PRICE:	UNDER $15,000	UNDER $20,000	UNDER $25,000
	96%	75%	62%

Surprising, right? Let's analyze the reasons for this phenomenon. It all started after World War II. Steel and aluminum became available. Manufacturers of trailers started constructing wider models of their products for use as permanent residences. In 1954, 76,000 units of these homes were sold. In 1957, the sales jumped to 119,300. In 1964, 191,320. In 1969, 412,690.

It's easy to understand. By 1960, inflation had pushed conventional housing prices through the ceiling. Prices were going up at a rate of 18 per cent yearly. At the same time, the need for housing had increased. Many couldn't afford to buy new conventional homes. Older homes were already occupied.

Automobile manufacturers kept making cars. More imaginative entrepreneurs, who made trucks and trailers, entered the housing market and met the insistent demand for low-price housing by building mobile homes in which couples could live.

More than 9 million Americans bought and lived in these "factory-produced" homes. One third of these homes were bought by retired couples. Prices began at less than $7,000 per unit. The mobile homes came fully furnished. The mobile home as sold included kitchen, bath, two or three bedrooms. They were generally sold equipped with appliances and furniture and wall-to-wall carpeting.

All the buyers had to do was to sell their own furniture. Then they gathered up their clothing, their dishes, their cherished knickknacks and moved in. They picked their mobile home parks, often in their own states, and became mobile home residents.

The reason for the low prices of mobile homes is understandable. An assembly line, in a controlled indoor environment, is easier and less expensive to manage than a site operation. An assembly line can turn out a complete mobile home from frame to draperies and accessories in less than an hour.

Put it this way. A site-built building is put together brick by brick or shingle by shingle. Construction crews of well-paid workers, usually unionized, take weeks—often months— to produce a house. A mobile home is manufactured inside a plant. Labor costs are 15 per cent of the wholesale costs. The materials are at hand inside the factory. They are literally stamped out by the machinery.

Building low-income homes through manufacturing and assembly processes became the only way to meet the burgeoning need for low-cost housing.

By 1973, there were about seven hundred manufacturers

of mobile homes in the United States and ten or twelve more in Canada. There was one manufacturer in Mexico.

All of these mobile home makers made money. So did the manufacturers of supplies and accessories. Likewise transportation companies who moved mobile homes to mobile home parks. Bank and finance companies made money, too. Interest rates on mobile homes were between 12 to 14 per cent.

In 1973, *Forbes* magazine ranked the three leading mobile home producers as to their profits. The top three mobile home makers ranked one, two and three as the *most* profitable corporations in the United States over the years from 1968 to 1973.

Barron's, the weekly business paper, reported in 1975, "Few, if any manufacturing groups enjoy more favorable and well-defined prospects for the long haul than mobile home makers."

Nothing in this world stands still. Things improve. Or they deteriorate. By now, there are mobile homes which have the appearance and conveniences of site-built homes. They are put down in mobile home parks which offer all the advantages and pleasures of "country club" living. They feature golf courses, swimming pools, a gracious social life, entertainment. Central areas are also available for the indulgence of hobbies, discussions and pleasant organized programs of various kinds.

These mobile homes sell for $40,000 and up. We aren't going to concern ourselves with them. The rich know how to live. They also know how to fight back if their properties turn out to be rip-offs.

Our interest is in the mobile homes of the less affluent. We need to analyze regular mobile homes built to comply with minimum A119.1 standards. These standards, however, have been set up by the federal government working with mobile home *manufacturers*.

We turn to the book *So You Want to Buy a Mobile Home* by Al Griffin (published in 1970 by Henry Regnery Company, Chicago, $5.95). According to Griffin, lower-price mobile homes deteriorate in value over seven years. A $7,000 mobile home, for example, is worth $2,900 after seven years. A $10,000 mobile is worth $4,100 after seven years.

Thus we discover a peculiar comparison. There is a shortage of site-built homes. This enhances the resale value of these structures even when jerry-built. Any regular home can be sold at a profit, often a substantial profit. A $15,000 house today resells for at least more than double its original price.

Most mobile homes deteriorate in value over seven years. That's because they are badly built. They are cheaply furnished. They are often located outside of cities, in areas where the few building codes are inadequately policed to protect the mobile home owners.

What sells mobile homes is "flash" and garish interior decoration. Chandeliers and "carved" cabinet fronts are made of molded plastic. Bars in living rooms are cardboard covered with vinyl. Bright, "satin" bedspreads are made of cheap synthetics.

But in the housing market today, there are few choices for the quite young and the newlyweds and for the retired. Our interest, of course, relates to the experiences of the aged who have purchased or who plan to purchase mobile homes.

We grow tired of caring for our big houses. We are beaten down by increasing property taxes. They eat into our low Social Security incomes. We are appalled by maintenance

costs, such as painting and repairs. More and more of us retirees buy mobile homes which we hope to use for the rest
of our lives.

We sell our properties at a profit and move. One retired
lawyer reported, "It's foolish to isolate from $25,000 to
$100,000 which is unproductive when you can duplicate
most of your living comforts for $8,000. The money I saved
by buying a mobile home is out earning something."

Such mobile home buyers can afford to be unconcerned
about seven-year deterioration. The high interest rates (mobile home loans 12 to 14 per cent) don't bother them
either.

Let's forget the rich. Our concern in this book is for
the less affluent retirees. They are the ones who spend a
large part of their life savings for a mobile home.

Back in 1975, the Center for Auto Safety conducted an exhaustive two-year investigation of the mobile home industry. Similarities between the manufacture, merchandising
and term payments of cars justified such an investigation.

"Like cars," the Center for Auto Safety explained, "mobile homes are factory-built on assembly lines. They are sold
through dealership networks. They are delivered with factory warranties."

They are registered and taxed as *vehicles* in most states.
They are issued license plates. They are financed through
high-cost installment contracts. Their hybrid status has
caused mobile homes to be ignored both by government officials responsible for regulating motor vehicles and by those
responsible for regulating housing.

The result of the Center for Auto Safety investigation produced a book entitled *Mobile Homes—The Low-Cost Housing Hoax.*

What had started the investigation were hundreds of letters which consumer advocate Ralph Nader had been receiving since 1971. These writers had no other place to turn for help.

For example:

> I sincerely hope you can help us, or at least do something that will scare these mobile home companies enough to quit this ruthless selling to people . . . especially to poor ones who, once they purchase—are stuck . . . with poorly constructed homes, and worse, with no one to correct these faults.

The complaint letters tell the story of a young industry whose interest in the safety, quality and service of its products has not kept pace with its rapid growth. Another mobile home owner wrote:

> We would have been ahead of the game by far if we had bought Champion stocks instead of buying a piece-of-junk Champion home in 1970. . . . If they would spend a few dollars more on their product instead of cheating the public, we'd be in less of a jam today. . . . I wish I had the patience to go into detail about all the things that have gone wrong to homes.

Hundreds of letters of this kind set up the agenda of the CFAS investigation. After the study was begun (in 1971), the Center (whose largest financial supporter is Consumers Union, publishers of *Consumer Reports*) worked independently of the Nader organization.

Now we are going to make a flat statement. *Don't buy a mobile home unless you've read this book. If you can't afford the $10.95 price get the book from your local library.*

If your library doesn't have it write to The Center for Auto Safety, 1223 DuPont Circle Building, Washington, D.C. 20036.

They produced a book called *Mobile Homes—The Low-Cost Housing Hoax.*

The early chapters tell us what a mobile home is, who buys them, how they are sold and merchandised.

Following chapters cover the wheeling and dealing on the mobile home sales lot. The types of dealerships are described. The prices of their products are given.

Many mobile home owners are left grumbling about the dealers who sold them their homes. Twenty-seven per cent of the mobile home owners interviewed in a 1970 survey conducted by the Owens-Corning Fiberglas Corporation said they "probably" or "definitely" would not buy another mobile home from the same dealer. Another 25 per cent felt dubious enough about their dealers to give an ambivalent response, saying they "might" buy again from the same dealer.

The Division of Consumer Protection of Ohio's Department of Commerce conducted a survey of new mobile home owners. Half of those who answered the questionnaire felt that certain statements made by sales personnel about their homes were false or misleading. They also reported that dealers failed to live up to promises made by their salesmen. Similarly, nearly one third of the mobile home owners who wrote to Ralph Nader and the Center for Auto Safety complained about their dealers' sales practices and servicing.

Please don't skip Chapter 4 of the *Hoax* book. It speaks for itself. Its title is, "Financing and Insurance." The subtitle of the chapter is "Doubling the Price of a Mobile Home

Without Even Trying." That's where your money can go up to 14.5 per cent on loans when you buy a mobile home.

Chapter 5, "Up Against the Zoning Wall," has a subtitle which reads "From Mudholes to Moburbia." A useful quote here: "More than half the people who buy mobile homes move into such parks. Once there, they find themselves part homeowner and part tenant—owners but not masters of their homes. They are impotent tenants who are often told when to water their grass, how late at night to use their televisions, and how many people may live in their homes. Excluded from existing tenant-landlord regulations in many states, mobile home park residents usually have fewer rights than apartment dwellers. Rarely are park residents granted leases; even worse, they are subject to being evicted without cause on a few days' notice.

Chapter 5 of the *Hoax* book provides a frightening description of the lopsided landlord-tenant relationship in some mobile homes. Here are details of some rental agreements. They substitute for leases. Or they may be offered as additional clauses in the lease. Please note that rental agreements in mobile home parks today are rarely subject to government scrutiny or regulation. Read the conditions and weep.

> Tenancy in many mobile homes may be terminated immediately by either party with or without cause simply by giving notice.

> For example: The contract of Chateau Rochester, one of the "luxury" mobile home communities built by Chateau Industries in Michigan, demands that renters read and sign the following:

"Chateau reserves the right to revise, add to or change rules and lot rental amounts, additional fees as deemed necessary for the continued maintenance of this fine residential community.

"I hereby agree to the terms and conditions set forth in the rules and regulations booklet or as it may be amended from time to time."

Note that these unfair conditions exist in *luxury* mobile home parks. Is it likely that conditions in less expensive mobile home parks will be less onerous?

Chapters 6 and 7 and 8 and 9 should frighten you. The titles are: Chapter 6, "The High Cost of Low Quality"; Chapter 7, "Run Around (What the Industry's Warranty and Service System Delivers Best)."

Chapter 8 is headed simply enough. "Keeping It Cheap and Inflammable." Chapter 9 is entitled "Huff, Puff, Blow Your House Down." If you value your life read these two chapters in *The Low-Cost Housing Hoax.*

Chapter 10 talks about "standard-setting and enforcement." "Is this," asks the chapter, "consumer protection? Or is it a public relations stunt?"

For anybody's money, the last chapter of the *Hoax* book is the best one in the book. It is an outline for action by the consumers, by the mobile home industry and by the government.

But this chapter leaves out one key factor which will be needed to clean up the mobile home mess. That is action by *elders themselves.*

Many of us may want to buy and own mobile homes. Where is the National Council on the Aging? What part should local branches of the National Council of Senior Citizens (NCSC) play in this struggle? Why have not the local branches of the American Association of Retired Persons (AARP) and the National Retired Teachers Association (NRTA) gotten into this effort to clean up mobile home practices? *Once more corrective action is up to us.*

We activist elders call for the creation of a public hearing by Senator Church of the Senate Committee on Aging and by Congressman Claude Pepper of the congressional Select Committee on Aging to expose mobile homes as possible threats to our later years. No such hearing has ever been held.

The book to read first on the subject is *Mobile Homes— The Low-Cost Housing Hoax* ($10.95), published for the Center for Auto Safety, 1223 DuPont Circle Building, Washington, D.C. 20036.

Your life, your money, your comfort in your old age may depend on reading this book.

Postlude

Readers deserve the right to evaluate those issues about which Nikka and I were at odds. What better place is there for this than the final chapter of this book?

Nikka believes that the book requires a discussion of how politics affects the lives of elders. "National, state, county and local services to the elderly," she said, "are tied into political considerations."

"So far you're right," I agreed. "Older citizens cast ballots in more elections than do most Americans," I added.

"Aren't we elders the last group of Americans who think of voting as a sacred privilege as well as a duty?" she asked.

"Agreed again," I answered.

Nikka continued, "But your book makes no recommendations about how we can use our votes in the interest of our age group."

"Are you suggesting that it makes a difference to the elderly whether the Republicans or the Democrats get into office?" I countered. "What I say is, a plague on both their houses."

"Wrong thinking there. Wrong emphasis, too," Nikka answered. "It's not a question of party voting. In fact, it's a problem of selecting candidates *without* regard to political party affiliation."

"Some job *that* will be," I interrupted. "Candidates for office—any office—make promises they either can't keep or don't intend to keep. Individual promises are keyed to the party line which offers gold in the streets to every sector of the population."

She admitted that the issue was not a matter of Republicans and Democrats. However, she added another angle to the discussion.

"Isn't it safe enough to assume that candidates who are largely conservative in their thinking will do less for the elderly and the needy than more progressive candidates?" Nikka queried.

"True enough," I said. "I'll agree that when it comes to an 'aye' vote or a 'nay' vote on expenditures for social programs, conservatives will usually vote against such spending."

Nikka pressed on. "And aren't we elders among the people who are *most* in need of special programs?"

"We are indeed," I agreed. "But the conservative legislator usually represents a more affluent district. Even the elderly in such a district agree that money spent for social purposes comes out of their pockets."

"All the more reason for uging them to vote for progressive-minded candidates," she replied. "Along the line somewhere, their comforts are at risk. Well-to-do they may be now. But they all know that one major sickness, for example, could wipe them out. The lack of a national health plan that works like the ones in other industrial countries is as important to them as it is to the average American older person."

"I accept that," I said. "But doesn't this warning come through in my book? In a sense, the entire content of the book is political. If readers don't get the message, my telling them how to vote will be a waste of time."

"Not so," she countered. "One of the main objectives of the book is to get pre-retired and younger people to understand what they'll be up against when they're old. You're not going to pin down this concept without specific arguments against political conservativism."

Nikka turned to other matters. Later she picked up her recorder and practiced for a while. I considered what she had said. Finally, I interrupted her music playing and asked, "Why don't we leave this discussion for readers to decide?"

"How can we do that?" she asked.

"Well, we both believe that conservative politicians resist the idea of helping the needy, the sick, the old and the helpless. Some conservatives are more negative than others. I'm reluctant to make or even to suggest voting *decisions* for other elders. All I'm trying to do with this book is to explore the facts about the quality of our lives during our years as elders," I said.

"So what's your plan?" she asked.

"I'll describe this particular disagreement in the book. I'll report honestly on the discussion we had. Let the readers determine which one of us is right."

Nikka in turn thought about this idea. "Pretty sneaky," she said with a smile. "You're just afraid to tackle the question of politics and how it affects us oldsters."

I smiled back at her. "Afraid? No. Lazy might be a better word."

Nikka accepted that without comment. Then she said, "You haven't covered the special problems of widows or widowers either."

"You may remember that I tried to get information on that phase of our lives," I answered. "But I pulled a blank."

"What happened?" she asked.

I glanced at my notes. "Widows and widowers to whom I spoke gave me no help at all. But I made a great discovery."

"Namely?"

"Dead husbands and dead wives all become angels."

"How do you mean that?"

"You won't believe this, Nikka. Not one widow or widower had anything bad to say about a former spouse now deceased."

She asked, "Would that include Joe W., who as we know was a mean so-and-so? And a male chauvinist to boot. He treated his wife Sally like a servant."

I said, "It also included Mary S., whom we knew as a first-class harridan. She drove her husband Charlie to his grave. It seems the deceased are all described by former spouses as having been perfect mates."

"Cite me an example."

I read from my notes. "Mary said Charlie was a beautiful person. Joe W. said, 'I don't expect ever to meet a more understanding woman than Sally. She was a blessing for me and our kids.'"

Nikka smiled. "How do you explain such responses?"

"My interpretation is that nobody wants to admit that a long marriage was full of Sturm and Drang."

"I have a different thought," Nikka suggested. "They

might have hoped that their deceased spouses might intercede for them with God."

"So, my wise wife, how do I write a chapter on widows and widowers?"

We were both silent for a while. Then I had an idea.

"Nikka," I asked, "would you object if I described some of the facts of our own lives together? You're seventy-four years old. I'm seventy-five. Barring a catastrophe, one of us will die before the other. You know we've thought about this. We've tried to anticipate each other's situation as relicts."

"So we have," she admitted. "You have my permission to describe what we do. Can you explain our thinking on the matter by citing an example of action?"

"I think I can. We both agree that in case of death, the important thing is to prepare the relict to be self-sufficient in practical matters."

"So far you're right."

I continued. "And did we not decide that since I never learned how to cook, I should be prepared at least to cook a proper meal for myself if you died first?"

"That's right. You're doing fine in that area."

I pressed on. "And didn't I convince *you* that there would be money problems you'd be required to handle if *I* died first?"

"You did."

"So now I can cook a proper meal," I boasted.

"And much as I hate it, I can make deposits, check investments and pay bills and control money matters as well as you can," Nikka said proudly.

"That's true," I agreed. "But it did take you forty-four years of marriage before you undertook such chores."

"And how many years did it take you to learn the simple rules of how to prepare a roast?" she countered.

"Touché," I said.

We left the discussion at that. We have our separate interests and enthusiasms. We've done what we could to prepare one another for life if the other died.

Of course, what we've done goes beyond cooking and money matters. But readers will get the idea. Whichever of us dies first, the one who remains will still be a whole person.

That's a comforting thought.

Index